FEARLESS. INSPIRED. TRANSFORMED.

F. I. T.

FOR SUCCESS

ALL THINGS ARE POSSIBLE
IF YOU KEEP GOING

ADREAN TURNER

SOUND WISDOM
P.O. Box 310
Shippensburg, PA 17257-0310

For more information on publishing and distribution rights, call 717-530-2122 or info@soundwisdom.com.

Quantity Sales. Special discounts are available on quantity purchases by corporations, associations, and others. For details, contact the Sales Department at Sound Wisdom.

While efforts have been made to verify information contained in this publication, neither the author nor the publisher assumes any responsibility for errors, inaccuracies, or omissions.

While this publication is chock-full of useful, practical information, it is not intended to be legal or accounting advice. All readers are advised to seek competent lawyers and accountants to follow laws and regulations that may apply to specific situations.

The reader of this publication assumes responsibility for the use of the information. The author and publisher assume no responsibility or liability whatsoever on the behalf of the reader of this publication.

ISBN 13 TP: 978-1-937879-95-2
ISBN 13 Ebook: 978-1-937879-96-9

For Worldwide Distribution, Printed in the U.S.A.
2 3 4 5 6 7 8 / 20 19 18

Cover/Jacket designer Eileen Rockwell
Interior designer Terry Clifton

*I dedicate this book to my wonderful, loving husband,
Richard, who encourages me every day. And to my
parents, Andrew and Lizzie Jackson for instilling in me
the confidence to pursue my dreams. And my sister, Angela
who is a true example of beauty, strength, and courage.*

*I also dedicate this book to my children, Angelique,
Richard IV, and Jordan. I pray that you follow your dreams
and live out loud to make the best of the blessing of life.*

CONTENTS

INTRODUCTION

The wisdom in this book has been accumulated and compiled from my popular podcasts heard on national and international channels. Divided into six parts, each concise, bite-sized, blog-style chapter is jammed with practical and precise principles for moving you forward toward success in your personal and business life.

As a certified career coach, speaker, professional development trainer, and business consultant, I have twenty-five years of experience in management, marketing, operations, teaching, and training to partner with individuals, entrepreneurs, and organizations to achieve their maximum potential.

FIT for Success reveals important information and inspiration to keep you going through everyday situations at work, at home, and in your personal quiet time. Are you looking for a better way to engage with your boss, coworkers, and family members? You will find that better way within the following pages.

If you need support to achieve more or feel stuck in your career, you can slide into a new and exciting lifestyle of success by absorbing the advice provided.

Would you like to build community, spark inspiration, and boost attendance at your business or social gatherings—and even the dinner table? All things are possible with these proven, common sense strategies that will help you to excel in your career, business—and life.

You can be different—be uniquely you—and still fit with others when you are fearless, inspired, and transformed.

PART I

PERSONAL & BUSINESS DEVELOPMENT

START Me Up!

In this journey called life we are often faced with so many decisions and demands that we live in a constant state of hurry. And we know that the more we rush, the higher the chances of failing. Especially in these frantic times, it's important to stay calm. If you find yourself running around in circles, *stop and implement the START formula*. This concept was developed by

Andreas von der Heydt to significantly reduce the risk of being dragged into situations where you might lose it. Choose it… START.

S—Stand up. You're not a pushover. Don't be afraid to say no, especially if you already have too much on your plate.

T—Trust. You know more than you think you do. Go with your gut when you're in a rut.

A—Action. Be strategic with your execution. That will help to eliminate distractions.

R—Respond and be Responsible. If you need help, be brave enough to ask for it. And…

T—Take it easy. Don't take yourself or your tasks too seriously. No matter how far behind you are or how badly you've messed up, relax. Failure is a bruise, not a tattoo.

When times are hectic, and they will be, keep in mind that the more relaxed you are in life, the more *powerful* you become. Use the START formula for greater success in managing challenging situations.

I Promise

Are you good at keeping your word? We often make promises to other people, but what about the promises you make to yourself? To live more successfully recall "The Promise" by Frank Sonnenberg.

Promise yourself to:

- Live every day to the max.
- Dream big and see every glass as half full.

- Set high expectations for yourself and for those around you.

- Get things done rather than talking about them.

- Say you'll try rather than complaining why you can't.

- Lead by example rather than through control.

- Win with integrity rather than at all costs.

- Make work fun rather than a chore.

- Face challenges head-on rather than surrendering your dreams to fear.

- Raise your hand rather than pointing your fingers.

- Learn from mistakes rather than covering them up.

On life's journey, promise yourself to do your best and nothing less. Make people feel good about themselves and proud of their accomplishments. Be as excited about the success of others as you are about your own. If you promise yourself anything less, you'll be letting yourself down.

Your promises have power—keep them. Commit to achieving *all* the things God has purposed for you. I promise you won't be sorry if you do.

From Wrong to Right

Are you facing a particular challenge that has you puzzled? You've dotted all the i's and crossed all the t's and things still aren't adding up? At times, despite our best efforts, things don't seem to be working in our favor.

This is the very dilemma one of my clients was facing. She made a decision to pursue her dream life. It seemed that as soon as she started progressing with her plan, the bottom fell out. The promotion she was counting on to have the extra dollars through the transition wasn't an option after the company reorganized under new management. She faced a physical illness and other setbacks and began to lose confidence.

Can I say I'm not surprised? When you decide to make a change, roadblocks seem to appear from nowhere. It happened to me. Instead of viewing it as a barrier, I chose to see it as a learning experience. It's like "the universe" is preparing you for the next step. If this is your story, know this: it will all work out for what's best for you! *Everything* happens for a reason.

These are only tests. And you will pass each one if you keep going. Journal about your journey. Write down how you're feeling, what you're going through, the actions you're taking, how you're transforming. Write the good and the not-so-good "stuff." It's all part of your story. And it will be a record of your perseverance—and a source of inspiration.

Consider this: sometimes everything is going wrong for all the right reasons. *You'll never know how strong you are until being strong is the only choice you have.* Stay focused and faith-filled—and you will succeed!

Career Boost or Bust

Statistics show that the average work week is now 44 hours. American workers spend long days and nights at the office or on remote devices to advance career opportunities. However the trade-off is the imbalance realized in your personal life. Yet, you can make great strides in your career using several small strategies.

To boost your career and increase your paycheck...

1. Be reliable. You have probably worked with employees who couldn't be trusted. There's always that one person who doesn't keep promises. Avoid establishing a similar reputation. If you say you're going to do something, do it.

2. A surefire way to gain your manager's attention is to always have your work done on time. Impress your boss by turning in assignments early.

3. And boost your career by dressing the part. Your physical appearance matters. Many promotions are given to the candidate who is dressed for success. Always dress up one level from your peers. You'll be surprised how much of a difference it makes.

4. When looking for opportunities of advancement, be indispensable. *Find an important task and master it.*

5. Is your company looking for volunteers to learn a new software program? Say yes and impress your management team.

6. Is a long-time employee leaving? Maybe you can fill the gaps created by the departure. This can help to distinguish you from your peers

and open pathways to a bigger paycheck and promotion.

While none of these strategies is likely to make a significant difference by itself, when combined, the results can be impressive.

Dealing with Discomfort

It is a fact of life that we will face trials and tribulations. They may manifest in the form of physical or emotional discomfort. Indeed, *most scientists believe that feelings of discomfort are attempts by our brain to keep us safe.* For instance, there's a reason you're afraid to jump off a cliff. However, there are times when your brain leads you astray. You can feel fear about a certain course of action, even if it is the best option.

Here's the question—are you going to let your brain control you, or are you going to control your brain?

To skillfully deal with the discomfort associated with decision-making try these methods:

- Ask yourself, *Is the discomfort I'm feeling legitimate?* Protecting your life and your source of income are examples of legitimate concerns. The fear felt before a public speaking engagement isn't. *Don't let discomfort limit you.*

- *Address your discomfort head-on.* If you're stressed about work, find ways to resolve the situation. If it can't be resolved, there's no point in worrying about it. Implement coping mechanisms such as prayer, meditation, or positive-thinking exercises.

- *Learn to be comfortable with discomfort.* You can get used to anything. Start small. For example, I decided to connect with one new person each week to build my online network. Now I have relationships with people I otherwise may have never met had I let my discomfort delay my growth. Start with a small area of discomfort. Then in time, you'll be able to handle higher levels of distress.

- *Realize that fear and anxiety are nothing more than a few chemicals coursing through your veins.* Those chemicals can be effective, but you don't have to give in to them.

Many people are successful only because of their ability to do things others are too uncomfortable to do. Let go of fear and activate your faith to squash discomfort in decision making and gain more success.

The Brain Train

The other day someone said to me, "Coach Adrean, I have been doing this positive thinking and affirmations thing, and it isn't working for me." Does that sound familiar?

Positive thinking and affirmations are a way of reprogramming your mind. And that can take time. Think about raising a child. You often say "No! Don't touch the stove. No, don't put that in your mouth. No, don't say that." We learn by the negative—so now we have to train our brains for the positive, YES.

Positive thinking is believing in yourself and your abilities. **Yes,** I can achieve that goal. **Yes,** I can resist that huge slice of chocolate cake. **Yes,** I can survive without a spouse in my life right now. **Yes,** I will ace the next job interview. **Yes,** I can make it!

In life, *believing in the positive* is half the battle. BUT the other half is *action*. Get in motion and stay in motion so you can see change in your life. That is not an overnight process. It will take time and practice. *Positive thinking must become a habit.* Follow the three P's:

PLAN. List the things that alter your mood and cause you to think negativity, then write down what you are going to do to combat those thoughts and emotions.

PRACTICE. One of my mood changers was the morning traffic. I used to be an impatient and fussy driver, so I had to change my mental response—especially when my children started driving and claimed they were emulating me. Embarrassing! Now I drive slower, smile more at other drivers, and just get out of the way. BUT I had to practice that. I even put a note on my dashboard: SLOW DOWN!

PREPARE. Are you are dealing with a challenging coworker? Or someone who gossips or is just plain annoying? What do you do? Change the atmosphere. Change the topic. Change the mood. If the person says, "This job is crappy," respond, "I enjoy my work." If the person says, "I'm afraid we're going to get laid off," respond, "If that happens, it'll give me time for reflection and a chance at another fulfilling opportunity."

You can train your brain. Positive thinking is having faith and living with the expectation of excellence always!

Busy Being

Time and time again we hear individuals speak of how busy they are as if it's a badge of honor. Maybe it makes them feel important or perhaps they are openly complaining. Whichever the case, *there's an epidemic of excessive busyness among adults that leaves us feeling rushed, discontent, and short on time.* If you're feeling swamped, it's time to create more balance in your life. Try these solutions for managing your time to become more productive.

1. **Solution 1:** *Live mindfully.* That means engage fully in whatever you're doing. Focus on one task at a time. You'll reduce stress and enhance the quality of your work.

2. **Solution 2:** *Choose your priorities.* Think about your purpose and devote your time to the activities that matter to you. Using your time wisely makes your life more meaningful.

3. **Solution 3:** *Manage your time better by establishing routines.* Do you spend as much time coordinating your work as actually performing it? *A systematic approach turns frequent chores into automatic habits, reducing the time accomplish tasks.*

4. **Solution 4:** *Collaborate with others.* Outsource or eliminate tasks to accomplish more.

Being busy and being productive are two different things. Be sure that you are focusing on the activities that will support your growth. You'll find that less can be more fulfilling.

Unlock and Block

Many people limit themselves, which impacts their ability to accomplish goals. *Most limiting beliefs are rooted in fear*—fear of rejection…of failing again…of not being good enough or talented enough.

To unlock your potential requires purposeful thought. You can unblock negative beliefs by following these:

- **Embrace your limitations.** You can't be everything to everyone and no one is perfect. There will always be someone smarter, stronger, or faster than you. Even if you're not the best at something, you can still be very successful, as long as you make an effort. *Don't allow the fear of inadequacy stop you from trying.* It's okay if you try and fail. Failure is a pathway to success.

- **Set clear goals.** Take time to think about and understand what you truly want to achieve and strategize step by step, goal to goal. Knowing your destination limits negative beliefs and provides encouragement as you journey through to accomplish them.

- **Be positive.** Things will be impossible if you *believe* them to be! Inspiration and motivation are the most powerful ways to defeat limiting thoughts. Surround yourself with encouraging people. Post uplifting information around your office. Believe the best. Positivity ignites passions.

Your mind is a powerful thing, when you fill it with positive thoughts, your life will start to change!

Endure

A coaching client was struggling with difficulty dealing with a certain situation and finding it challenging to move forward. She remarked that some people she thought would be there for her in her time of need had turned their backs leaving her feeling lost and discouraged.

To excel in life, you will have to endure through obstacles. The dictionary defines "endure" as a means to undergo without giving in. It means to carry on through despite hardships. It means DON'T GIVE UP! I often say that over the years through tears and fears, I have learned to endure. If you live long enough, you learn that you just have to hold on.

Ensure that you will ENDURE with these solutions:

- Determine what you can and cannot control. It's important to understand where your strength lies. Manage the things you can—and leave the rest to God. You don't have to solve all your problems. Some things will work themselves out if you let them.

- Be still. In the words of Iyanla Vanzant, "Listen for the solution instead of begging for direction. It will come to you when you need it. In the meantime, rest in the assurance."

- Surrender and detach. Let go of the situation. If you've harmed someone apologize and move on. And if they don't accept your apology, it is none of your business. If someone has harmed you. Forgive them. Let peace be your reward.

- Stop inviting folks to your pity parties. No one wants to receive a recurring invitation to that event. Instead of dwelling on the negative try focusing forward. The best is yet to come. Believe that to be true and it will happen.

A setback is a setup for a comeback. Affirm it. Proclaim, "I will live peacefully in the midst of my trials!"

Keep it Together

Someone once said the most expensive thing in the world is *trust*—it can take years to earn and just a matter of seconds to lose. If you find a person of trust, you have found a jewel.

The following are my top ten ways to support you in keeping it together to build trust and credibility with others for greater success:

1. Keep your word. Your promise should be as binding as a contract.

2. Keep your promises. Follow through on every commitment you make.

3. Keep good company. Surround yourself with people of high integrity.

4. Keep the peace. Learn how to disagree without being disagreeable.

5. Keep it simple! It's not only what you bring to the table, it's how you bring it.

6. Keep going! Good intentions are just the beginning!

7. Keep it in perspective. You gain more by making others look good than singing your own praises.

8. Keep it a secret! Words spoken in confidence are words spoken in trust.

9. Keep it honest! Admit when you are wrong.

10. Keep quiet! Be a good listener.

When you build trust, you build relationships and break-down barriers. Keep growing!

Begin Again

One weekend I found the clarinet my daughter used to play when she was in high school. It had been in a closet collecting dust for ten years. When she came for a visit, I showed it to her and she immediately assembled it and started playing. It was as if we had turned back in time. The melodies she played were sweet and we all stood around cheering.

I started to think. *What else have I put away, hidden in the closets that are waiting to be pulled out and put to use?* How about you? Is it a dream of going back to school or opening your own business or reconnecting with old friends or exploring a new talent? You can begin again!

Take these steps to revive your dreams and make sweet music of your own:

Step 1: *Make the Decision.* Your situation will not change until *you* do. Decide today, right now that you will do what's necessary to make things happen for you.

Step 2: *Know Your Direction.* Cultivate a plan with SMART goals. These are goals that are Specific, Measurable,

Attainable, Realistic, and have a Time component. For example, "I will contact my mentor or coach to schedule time in the next week to develop strategies that will help me reach my goals." Being specific and gaining support will help you achieve results faster.

Step 3: *Remove Obstacles.* Whether they be your own thoughts, other people, money, or resources, identify what is preventing you from moving forward. Then address them head-on and devise ways to eliminate them or work around them. Remember, this is your dream, your time, and your purpose.

The moment you start to wonder if you deserve better, *you do!* Don't stay stuck! Begin again and live life on purpose for your purpose.

Procrastination Exacerbation

Procrastination is the thief of time. Time is one of your most valuable assets that you don't own. We often say that it will get done *someday*. But someday is not a day of the week. If you've been delayed in making your way adopt these simple habits to abolish procrastination for good:

1. Eliminate all but the essential tasks. Ask yourself, *Which projects will benefit me the most and have the most impact on my life?* One of the problems of procrastination is that we're so overwhelmed we don't know where to start. Choose a few tasks to focus on, then eliminate, delegate, or put the rest off for a while.

2. Create accountability. Get others to help you. Promise someone that you'll turn something in

to them by a certain date, or that you'd like for them to make sure you finish a project by a certain time. The more people you have who are expecting you to complete a project, the more likely you are to get it done.

3. Focus on a small task to get moving and make this a daily habit. Taking on an overwhelming task can stop us dead in our tracks. Imagine looking up at a mountain and deciding whether you're going to climb it today or if you're going to watch television. You'll pick watching television every time. Instead of looking at the mountain, which could be a large project or assignment, look only at the next action step necessary for the task.

4. Set deadlines. Without deadlines, it's more challenging to get things done. Reasonable timelines are like the finish line in a race. The closer you get to the date, the more energy you have to complete the assignment.

5. Clear away distractions. This is very difficult because of all the electronic and smart devices that grab our attention. Disconnect; put your cell phone on airplane mode, schedule times to check your email, and clear your desk of clutter to limit distractions.

It's not easy to conquer procrastination, but it's possible. Stay focused and encouraged!

The Perfect Remedy

For most people, we strive to be better people morally, to do things that exemplify goodness in our lives and to support others who are struggling. But on that journey, we can fall into a state of feeling we have to be perfect. We feel that we must have everything together all the time. You are a perfectionist if you exhibit these behaviors:

1. You can't stop thinking about a mistake you made.

2. You are intensely competitive.

3. You have to do things perfectly, or not at all.

4. You demand perfection from other people.

5. You won't ask for help.

6. You will persist at a task long after other people have quit.

7. You are very self-conscious about making mistakes in front of other people.

Perfectionists frequently think what they do is never good enough, can carry higher levels of stress and anxiety, have increased risk of illness, and decreased levels of contentedness. How do I know? Because I'm a recovering perfectionist.

Overcoming perfectionism requires patience, courage, and support. Try these tips:

- **Increase awareness of self-talk.** Tune in to your thinking and start to identify unhealthy, all-or-nothing thoughts. Learn to substitute your automatic negative thoughts with more positive optimistic thoughts. Ask questions like, "Is there another way to think about this?" Or, "Are things really as bad as I'm thinking right now?" Or, "Does it really matter if I only get this document 80 percent right for now and get some feedback?"

- **Be realistic** and a little easier on yourself. Substitute perfectionism with healthy achievement.

- **Try to set strict time limits on projects and** move on to another activity when time is up. This technique reduces the procrastination that typically results from perfectionism.

- **Learn to deal with feedback and criticism.** Concentrate on being more objective, and learn to grow from your mistakes.

Always remember that you are uniquely and wonderfully made…flaws and all!

Are You Down with IDD?

After weeks of working with a client who decided to reinvent her career, I began to notice a common pattern that was hindering her from meeting her weekly goals. I diagnosed her with IDD. Intention Deficit Disorder (IDD), which is characterized by action without meaning or purpose. Some have defined IDD as a measure of the quality of your life—what you intend to do versus what you *actually do*.

When you suffer with IDD, your best intentions may not be realized until they are partnered with the "why" or the purpose. Without purpose, you lose the passion, the fire, for following through to reach your goals. If you are being held down with IDD and want to improve the quality of your life and decrease these experiences:

- *Plan ahead.* Think about something you will purposefully do to enjoy the day. Whether it's enjoying your favorite dessert, mediating, or spending time with encouragers, make sure to plan to do something that will add light to your path.

- *Recognize the good in yourself.* This is an area that perfectionists struggle with. Don't be your own worst critic—be your own best motivator. Remind yourself of the things you do well versus the thing you messed up. Let that be the driver of your emotions to follow through on your intentions.

- *Set a goal* with a specific intention to help someone else. That is an expedient way to keep IDD at bay. Dedicating time to serve others within or outside your home or business will enrich your life. When you help others, you also help yourself.

- *Position yourself for success!* You may not accomplish all that you set out to do, but even the planning of your intentions can bring joy and improve your life!

Reach for the Moon

We've all heard the saying, "Reach for the moon, and if you miss, at least you land among the stars." At some point in your life, someone probably made that statement to you indicating that you have a lot of potential. But what good is potential if you don't capitalize on it?

For out-of-this-world results, implement these star-studded strategies:

- It's not just hard work that matters, but rather hard, smart work. Working hard on things that don't matter won't help anyone reach their highest potential. Ensure you're spending your time on important activities that challenge you to be your greatest you.

- Keep your eyes open. We get stuck in the same mental routines and fail to see all the opportunities around us. *An open mind is crucial to reaching your full potential.*

- Work on your strengths. Spend time fully developing your ability to apply your strengths to all aspects of your life. If you're a great organizer, volunteer to create an event for the youth in your neighborhood or present a topic of your passion at your next team meeting.

- Be assertive. Being passive is rarely an effective strategy. The squeaky wheel *does* get the oil—*ask for what you want.* You've got a 50 percent chance of a yes response. Let favor be your route to fortune.

It's not rocket science, but you're the astronaut of your life. Reach for the moon—spread your wings and fly. You never know what you can do until you give it a try. *Become the best possible version of yourself for greater success.*

Limitless

Do you put limitations on yourself, often finding reasons to quit a task before you even get started? It is not uncommon. As rational thinkers, our habits are to find ways to achieve our goals, but most times it's easier to find reasons why something may not work versus the joy and accomplishment we could derive from achieving success. A limiting mindset may stem from a difficult childhood, low self-esteem, or past failures. Yet, despite your specific reason, it all boils down to fear.

Unlock your potential and overcome your limitations with these tips:

- **Explore possibilities.** Sometimes things seem impossible for us, only because that's what we believe them to be. The battle is always in the mind. Focus on what you can do and believe the best for your next steps. You'll be amazed at how things will work out for your good.

- **Work a little harder.** Thomas Edison said, "Genius is 1 percent inspiration and 99 percent perspiration." Even coming up with a great idea for a new invention is more about hard work than about being brilliant. Lots of people are talented, but it takes someone who's willing to put in the extra effort to make it successful. Just get to work and do your best.

- **Get into position.** Before you get in your car and turn on the ignition, you have a destination in mind. Accomplishing things in life can be the same way. Have a clear understanding of where you want to go, and then you can figure out how to get there. Step out of your comfort zone and step into the fulfillment zone.

- **Open your mind** and overcome the obstacles blocking your potential. Turn "I wish" into "I WILL" and live beyond your limits!

Take a moment and write down a success you've achieved through limitless living. Let it serve as motivation for a prosperous journey of adventure.

Be Happy

In 1988, Bobby McFerrin became an overnight sensation for his song, "Don't Worry, Be happy." It was a simple message but a powerful mantra. With daily trials and challenges, happiness can sometimes seem distant. If you want more joy in your life, practice these three habits:

1. Express gratitude. Being thankful and appreciative creates an inner peace and solace that radiates a cheerful spirit.

2. Practice kindness. Joyce Meyer, an evangelist, often says, "if you want to find happiness find someone to bless". Selflessly helping someone is a super powerful way to change your perspective and someone else's too.

3.   Savor life's joys. Deep happiness cannot exist without slowing down to enjoy the special moments of life. Be grateful for the things you have now and people who support you.

Don't put off your joy. I've heard people say, "I'll be happy when we pay off the house...or when I get a new job...when I retire." What if tomorrow never comes? Happiness starts with you—not your relationships...not your job...not your money...but with *you*. Decide today, despite any obstacles you are facing, that you will enjoy the day and keep your attitude that way.

Life is full of choices. *Choose* happiness!

Think on Purpose

Have you ever started your day with anxious feelings, negative thoughts, and wish you could hit the "reset button" and start your day over feeling good? You don't have to be a hostage of your thoughts. Harvard Medical School research shows that 40 percent of what determines our happiness is under our control, another 10 percent is based on "good fortune". This means we have the power to improve our emotional well-being, no matter life's circumstances.

Here are some simple tips to mastering your thoughts so they don't control you:

■   Begin by *thinking on purpose.* Be aware of the thoughts that are passing through your consciousness—both the positive and the negative. Did you know that on average, we are bombarded with "65,000 thoughts a day, 95 percent of which are the same thoughts we have had the days before?" This tells us that our thought patterns become well-ingrained habits. By redirecting your thought pattern, you can change your perspective, responses, and actions.

- Break the habit of harmful thoughts by *rejecting the inclination to dwell on the negative.*

- In any given situation, you can choose to focus on what is right or what is wrong, and either way, you will be able to find evidence that supports what you are looking for. So, when a negative thought arises such as: "Today is not going to be a good day," or "I'm not good enough," or "No one cares about me," - challenge the messaging and replace it with a more compassionate and positive statement.

- An idle mind is the devil's workshop. Speak out loud to drown out your thoughts and change the channel to more affirming thoughts, visions, and feelings.

You don't have to believe everything you think. Be conscious of what you are saying to yourself because those are the most important words that matter.

Habit Havoc

Some habits are good, like eating healthy, exercising, helping your neighbors. But some habits cause havoc in our lives. They can result in overthinking, underperforming, or a medical or mental illness.

Studies show it takes at least twenty-one days to eliminate a bad habit and create a new, positive habit. Discipline is the bridge between goals and achievement. *Repeat* and practice your new habits consistently and daily to grow.

Then *replace* your bad habit with something else. If you're trying to be more positive when negative thoughts arise, recite affirmations or inspirational quotes. If you're trying to eat healthier, replace snacks with fruit. Think about what your bad habit gives you and find a replacement that provides the same benefit.

Remove your triggers. If you smoke, stay away from the places where you always smoked. If you're trying to save money, cut up your credit cards and avoid the places that tempt you to spend money. *Habits don't have a lot of thought behind them, they're almost like reflexes.* Don't put yourself in harm's way.

Bad habits are like a comfortable bed. They are easy to get into, but hard to get out of. Good habits are just as addictive as the bad, but much more rewarding. Set your mind on success and do your best!

Interrupt or Stay Stuck?

Do you have a habit of entertaining bad ideas, engaging with the wrong people, making the same mistake over and over, or pursuing limiting opportunities? If you want different results, it's likely that you need to interrupt the pattern of your thinking and behaviors or you will stay stuck. The following are four ways to move forward for your success:

1. It's important to *maintain a healthy mindset*. It's difficult to make the best decisions when your

mind is cluttered. When your thinking is stinking, you will likely stay stuck.

2. *Avoid spending major time on minor issues.* Know what's important and what needs your attention. Address only the things that will lead you closer to your goals.

3. *Turn your wounds into wisdom*—learn from your mistakes and poor choices. When faced with a similar situation you'll be better prepared to manage it and stay on track.

4. *Pause in the pursuit.* Too often we get caught up in the process of *doing* and lose sight of our purpose. Reflect on how situations influence you; realize when it's time to let go so you can grow. Refocus and keep moving forward!

Change isn't always comfortable, but if you always do what you've always done, you're likely to get the same results. Sometimes the simplest adjustments in your thinking can make a big difference for your success.

Take the Wheel

Do you sometimes dread walking into the office because you are dealing more and more with office politics that have nothing to do with your job description? Who's getting the promotion? Who's backstabbing who this week? Or perhaps, even worse, you skip the family get together because you just can't deal with the drama?

Many people prefer to avoid confrontation altogether, but that's not necessarily the best route for retaining close personal and professional relationships. Working through a conflict can actually build stronger relationships. How you address situations is what matters most. Take the wheel and gain control. It's time to decide; speak up or let it slide. Use these suggestions to determine your direction:

- *Don't sweat the small stuff.* If your husband left dirty dishes in the sink or your coworker was late to the meeting again, it may be more productive to focus on maintaining the positive dynamic you have with those individuals and to ignore the little things. Sometimes the issue that's bugging you isn't actually as important as preserving the relationship.

- *Practice the "Rule of 3."* Look for a pattern. Everyone slips up once in a while—but if the problem or issue is repeated three times, it's likely a behavior trend and it's time to bring it up. If there is a pattern, you'll know that a discussion is necessary.

- *Assess the damage.* Figure out if the issue you want to confront is legit—or just a difference of opinion. Ask yourself, *Does this person's behavior harm my family, my company, or me? Does it cost me something—like time or money? Or is it just annoying?* Check yourself before you wreck yourself.

- *Acknowledge your role.* There are different sides to every story. Admit your faults; focus on how the action made you feel or how you perceived it, rather than the other person's actions. That will put the other person at ease for a more calming discussion.

- *Timing is everything.* Avoid conflicts when you're still feeling upset about it, right before you've eaten, or at the end of a long day. When we are hungry, angry, lonely, or tired, we often don't behave our best. Therefore, we may not handle the situation in an appropriate manner.

Your goal is to create an atmosphere that is productive for you to excel. You'll do well when you decide what's best to address and move on. You're in the driver's seat. Go!

Fail to Win

It's no secret and most won't admit it, but the reason some people don't succeed in achieving their dreams is due to a fear of failure. The fear of failing keeps people in a stagnant state that causes unhappiness and restlessness. But in order to *win,* sometimes you have to *fail.*

Some of my most successful clients are individuals who have failed and pursued a new direction, or a new way of doing things, or a different way of seeing their opportunity. Some are retired from work but don't want to be retired from life. And other clients have decided that they want to pursue the things they love, that are soul-fulfilling.

The truth is, everyone will fail and we all make mistakes… it's inevitable. But there is a benefit to failing if you are open to learning. In many instances failure brings out the best in people:

1. *Failure leads to innovation.* Some of the greatest inventions and discoveries were born out of mistakes—penicillin and the smallpox vaccine are two examples.

2. *Failure allows you to identify your weaknesses.* **Therefore, you can work on making them strengths and know when you need to seek support.**

3. *Failure helps you gain perspective.* It humbles you and makes you more realistic about your goals.

Through it all, failure helps you make more informed decisions when you acknowledge them. So don't be afraid to fall down—just be sure you get up. And look where you slipped, not where you landed.

You've got to fail to win, but you first have to *begin!* Believe in yourself and make your goals and dreams come true.

Learn and Grow

If you think you'll reach an age in life when you don't have to learn anything new, you'll miss out on many enriching experiences. Aging experts insist that learning something new keeps our minds and mental health in better shape.

Maybe you get home after work and think, "I'm too tired to do anymore thinking today." You might be pleasantly surprised at how you can rest some areas of your mind while giving other areas a good work-out!

Don't wait until you get home. Expand your learning through listening to podcasts or instructional learning programs as you drive in your car or ride the bus, or train. Many books on audio are available at the library and can be loaned to you at no cost online.

Another idea is to join a club that focuses on a subject that interests you. Although I am a girly girl, I enjoy working on home projects. Often, you'll find me at a local home improvement store workshop learning about shelving, tiling, or gardening.

Have you ever thought about learning a new language to broaden your horizons? Educational software like Rosetta Stone is a great way to explore. Do you like parks and national monuments but don't have the money or time to visit? Check out tools like National Geographic's Explorer 3D that provides 3D maps of national parks. What you can learn at home on your computer with a good software program is pretty much unlimited.

Make it your personal mantra to never stop learning. It's fun, it will keep your mind working, and you'll never run out of fodder for interesting conversation. Stay open to the wonders of learning for the rest of your life. You'll enjoy the results!

Say No and Grow

Are you overwhelmed, overworked, tired, or worn down? If you answered yes, then it's probably time for you to say, "NO." No to that extra assignment at work. No to volunteering for every committee at church. No to dropping off and dragging the kids all over town for events and functions. It's sometimes hard telling others no, but saying yes may lead you to a mental and physical mess.

Saying yes makes you lose time doing things you really want (or need) to do and you can even become resentful toward the other person and yourself. Telling others that you can't acquiesce to their request doesn't have to be difficult. If you struggle to say no, try these quick tips:

- Explain! Let people know that you have other commitments. It might help to go into a little detail about the other things you have going on to increase their level of understanding.

- Inform! If you're in the middle of something, tell them that you'll get back to them. If what they need is really is urgent, they'll find someone else and shouldn't feel resentful toward you.

- Be decisive! If someone is trying to sell you something, tell the person that the offering doesn't meet your needs, but you'll get back to them if your needs change. This puts an end to the matter quickly without the other person feeling insulted. After all, you're rejecting their product or service; you're not rejecting them personally.

- Be resourceful! If you can't or aren't willing to get involved, refer them to someone else who would be a better help. Providing a suggestion may help the person gain the support they need.

Now practice. After you get used to saying no, you'll be surprised how easy it is and how receptive others can be. If you learn to say no to the things that you really don't want to do, don't have the time to do, or don't fit your needs, your life will be much richer for it.

Workaholic

True to the song, "Work" made famous by Rihanna, we live in an era that seems to celebrate a workaholic lifestyle. Think about how many people you've heard practically brag about staying up all night working or never taking a vacation day. The mentality boggles the mind.

Numerous studies have shown that a person's productivity goes down significantly long before many people call it quits for the day. If you're working a lot of hours, you're probably getting a lot less done per hour than many of your fellow employees.

Prevent work from taking over your life.

- Put a limit on your workday, like going home at 6 p.m. Or put a limit on a specific task, like one hour. Having a schedule helps you to focus, too.

- Maybe you're working all hours of the night because you're wasting too much time being distracted by online social activities. Disconnect at work. While some tasks require an internet connection, there aren't many. *When it's time to work - work. Then when it's time to have fun, enjoy it!*

- Spend less time working and get more done by allocating most of your time on the most important tasks. It's been proven that 20 percent of our work provides 80 percent of our results. Increase your "available" time by knowing where to focus your efforts most.

- Ask people for advice from those who have a great work-life balance. You don't always have to reinvent the wheel. Get some pointers for direction and clarity.

- Too much time at work negatively affects your relationship with your family and friends. Remember, no one says on their deathbed, "I wish I had spent more time at work." In the long run, family is always a priority.

- Avoid falling into the workaholic trap. Set a schedule and stick to it. With some intention and experimentation, you can get your work done and still get home at a reasonable hour.

You get what you work for and believe in. Believe you can and you will!

Forgive Yourself

When I look back over my life there were some things I did growing up that I regret and some that took a long time to heal. I realized that the problem I had with moving on with certain situations was because I am my own worst critic, and therefore hardest on myself.

That's common; the most difficult person for us to forgive is usually ourselves. Regret, shame, and guilt prevent us from letting go of our past mistakes.

Let go of blaming and start gaining more fulfillment. Move forward more quickly using these three simple strategies:

1. Be honest with yourself and others, and hold yourself accountable. Clearly identify what you did or didn't do, and own up to it. Examine the circumstances that led to your faux pas and be honest about how you felt then and how you are feeling now. Talk about it with someone you trust. It's likely that they'll see your mistake in a more forgiving light than you do.

2. Remedy the situation and make amends. Consider what you could have done and *develop a plan to act differently if you face a similar situation in the future.* If you had hurt others, offer an apology. That alone can be very healing—for them and you. If you're unable to make amends, consider acts of kindness to show that you truly regret your actions.

3. Realize that you've grown and you're no longer the same person who made the original slip-up. Continue to seek ways to help others and avoid actions that might lead to a similar lapse of judgment in the future. Your future can be greater than your past.

Forgive, live, and grow! Be true to yourself and find favor in your future!

A Clear View Will Do

There's a story of a young couple that moved into a new neighborhood. The next morning while they were eating breakfast, the young woman saw the neighbor hanging out the laundry. She remarks, "That laundry isn't very clean, she doesn't know how to wash laundry correctly, perhaps she need better laundry soap." The husband looks on, remaining silent. Every time the neighbor hangs out her laundry to dry, the young woman makes the same comments.

A month later, the woman is surprised to see nice clean laundry on the line and says to her husband, "Look, she's finally learned how to wash correctly. Do you think someone taught her?" The husband replies, "I got up early this morning and cleaned our windows."

And so it is with life, what we see when watching others depends on the clarity of the window through which we look. Sometimes we don't see things as they are—we see things as *we* are. The husband noticed the real issue and implemented a solution. Your life will be enhanced if you focus on solving problems and not just talking about them.

With the right perspective, clarity of objectives, and determination, you can achieve what you believe.

Small Wins

Most people achieve success one experience at a time. Comedian and talk show host Steve Harvey said that he is "a 20-year overnight success." Leaders from Bill Gates to Barbara Cochran attest that they were able to reach their career goals by individual steps or small wins.

Business experts and social scientists agree that modest victories provide major motivation to stay engaged along the journey of success. Per the "progress principle," based on a multi-year study by researchers at Harvard Business School, of all the things that can boost emotions, motivation, and perceptions, the single most important factor is making progress in meaningful work. And the more frequently people experience that sense of progress, the more likely they are to be creatively productive in the long run. Whether they are trying to solve a major scientific mystery or simply produce a high-quality product or service, everyday progress—even a small win—can make all the difference in how they feel and perform.

> *People who succeed have momentum. The more*
> *they succeed, the more they want to succeed,*
> *and the more they find a way to succeed.*
> —TONY ROBBINS

Try these steps to success to achieve your best:

Create. According to the Harvard team, one factor that encourages small wins is related to how you work. The catalyst factor includes events that directly enable progress in the work. These actions include developing clear goals, managing your time and resources effectively, and practicing open communication to influence productivity.

> *Surround yourself with only people*
> *who are going to lift you higher.*
> —OPRAH WINFREY

Relate. A second factor that encourages small wins is "nourishers." Interpersonal support can ignite and expedite your progress. Build relationships with colleagues and mentors who provide validation and constructive feedback. Nourishers can have a powerful influence on your performance. Involvement in personal or professional groups aligned with your mission and goals will enable you to cultivate those interactions.

Dictate. Keep a record of your accomplishments and setbacks. Maintaining a journal of your activities will help you recognize and celebrate miniature milestones that you might otherwise overlook. Tracking your advancement provides clarity to recognize conditions that affect your performance.

Success doesn't always come from the
big actions we take, but from the sum
of the small actions we repeat.
—ROBERT COLLIER

State. Considering the challenges of a large project can be overwhelming. Develop an action plan with intermediate goals. Break your assignment into small, manageable tasks. You'll become energized each time you accomplish a goal.

Use the small win strategy for your grand visions to achieve the success you desire for a fulfilling career.

Decisions for Your Life's Mission

One day I decided to try a new mascara. It had been advertised as something that would give me thicker, fuller, more luscious lashes. I usually hesitate to try new products because of my allergies, but I decided to try it anyway. And boy did I pay for that decision. My eyes became itchy and red and swelled. And although my pain was short-lived, it's an experience I won't soon forget.

This story is a simple analogy of things we do every day. We make decisions. Some decisions provide opportunities. Some come with risks. And some will change the course or condition of our lives. I encourage you to make decisions and take advantage of opportunities to grow, learn, travel, and build new relationships and create new experiences in your life.

Despite unhappiness being reported by 80 percent of American workers, only 50 percent of these workers reported taking time away from their jobs. And others have vacation days left at the end of the year.

It's time to make decisions for your life mission. Before I met my husband I never parasailed or attended a sporting event in an arena, much less watched a basketball or football game on TV. But sharing these experiences with him has brought so much joy into my life—because I was willing to try new things and didn't hesitate when presented with opportunities to spend time with him and explore new endeavors.

Decide today to create excitement in your life. Don't be afraid, even if you might feel a little pain. You're never too old, too settled, or too busy to become what you might have been.

The Ostrich Problem

Imagine that you're working on a new project or undertaking a new exercise routine. Perhaps you haven't been keeping tabs on how many milestones you've achieved or how much weight you've lost. You've got a vague sense of your progress, but you don't really know whether you're on schedule. Sound familiar?

If you responded yes, then you're likely suffering from The Ostrich Problem. The Ostrich Problem, is the tendency to avoid information about your progress toward goals.

Yet keeping track of your progress in a structured way is paramount to your success. Research shows that regularly monitoring your progress on any task puts you in a good mood and helps you aim toward progress.

Let go of the fear that you might not be on the right track and find out where you are. Remember, struggles and setbacks are part of the process. So ask a colleague to provide you with feedback on your progress at work, or keep a schedule of your progress, or simply self-check by asking yourself, *Am I moving forward, or just spinning my wheels?*

Keeping track allows you to see exactly how much is on your plate, not only day-to-day, but consistently over time. And if you haven't been tracking your progress, forgive yourself; but the longer you stick your head in the sand, the harder it can be to pull it out.

As Will Rogers said, "Even if you're on the right track, you'll get run over if you just sit there." Keep pushing forward. And stay the course. You'll notice that you will accomplish more and achieve greater success toward your goals.

Mistakes: Make 'em and Break 'em

Making mistakes is not a bad thing—if you *grow* from them. The following are five things I've learned from my mistakes:

1. Trust your instincts because they're almost always right. If something doesn't feel or look right, there's probably a reason. Let your experiences and intuition be your guide.

2. Take your time. Good decision-making requires perspective, and perspective comes with time. Most decisions can wait.

3. Don't waste your time on the wrong people. Most people aren't willing to take a chance on something outside their comfort zone. Don't spend major time with minor people. Seek individuals who share your visions for success.

4. Realize when things aren't meant to be. If you push too hard, all the time, you'll become vulnerable to mistakes. Discernment comes with wisdom.

5. Pick up the phone. Many mistakes and misunderstandings can be avoided through live conversations.

Make mistakes…then break the pattern because your best teacher is your last mistake.

Supersmart Start

Perhaps you've considered the success of Oprah Winfrey, Warren Buffet, or Mark Cuban and thought that they must be super smart. Have you thought that the super smart people are in their own private club? One that you could never penetrate? That doesn't have to be the case. To relate and become a card-carrying member, start practicing these three habits:

1. Supersmart people "know when to hold them and when to fold them." If you're on the wrong road, success means turning around and getting on the right path. Learn to make tough decisions.

2. Supersmart people don't guess. They read, research, and ask for advice before they make a decision. Do your homework.

3.   Supersmart people practice gratitude—regularly. It's the one attitude that has the biggest impact on success. When you are thankful for what you have, you'll end up having more. Schedule time daily to reflect and be grateful.

Sometimes old ways don't open new doors. Practice these behaviors of the supersmart for a successful start!

Fit Bit

Many people make a fitness goal resolution every New Year and then struggle to stay on track.

The challenge is that fitness can only be improved minimally from day to day, so it requires many days to really create a significant amount of improvement. And that's where we falter…we're unable to make a habit out of the behaviors that will make us fit.

To ignite your light in the fight for fitness, make fitness a daily part of your life.

It's tough to stick with your exercise routine if you do it alone. Find an exercise partner or join a team sport. When you can share the time with others, you have something else to focus on rather than how tired, sweaty, and bored you are. Look for Websites like Fitocracy.com to connect with other people in the same boat.

Find a way to enjoy the fitness journey. Take a Zumba class at the local YMCA, create a walking club with your coworkers, make it a contest with your family members to invigorate interest, excitement, and engagement.

Release the stress from the process. Keep things simple. Fight the temptation to have everything perfectly in place before you take a single step. Just throw on your shoes and go for a walk. Decide to skip the donut and have an apple instead. All fitness requires are simple decisions like these.

You don't need to plan your exercise routine for the next six months. You're not trying to launch the space shuttle; you're just trying to move around more than you have in the recent past.

Keep it social, fun, simple, and get it done. Make it a priority and proclaim your authority!

Tone Is Important

Ten percent of conflicts we experience are due to differences—90 percent are due to the wrong tone of voice. People hear your words but they feel your attitude based on your tone. Communicating passionately, quietly, or angrily impacts how people interpret you and what you're saying.

To win with words, ensure that your tone—the inflection, expression, and volume of your voice—demonstrates warmth, your expertise, sense of humor, and any other attribute you want to display.

Your tone is what makes you different and will attract others to you versus away from you. Keep in mind that when individuals identify a tone, they are also identifying a personality. They start to form an image of you based on your tone. By doing this, they feel as if they are getting to know you, the brand or the company you represent, bringing with it a sense of trust and familiarity.

Developing a consistent tone makes you seem more genuine and makes others feel at ease. That familiarity is comforting as they then know what to expect from you. And once you've gained trust, you have the power to influence others' decisions and persuade them to do business with you, partner with you on projects, or invest in opportunities that will benefit your career and the things you value most.

You've heard this before, "It's not what you say. It's how you say it that matters." Win with words by using a tone that doesn't leave you all alone.

Feast on Gratitude

Although most people celebrate the winter holidays with joy, that season is also one of the most stressful and depressing for many others. The family gatherings, endless parties, and shopping can really get some people down. That's why I encourage clients to feast on gratitude. One of the best ways to appreciate and improve your life is to experience the joy and excitement each day brings through an *attitude of gratitude.*

Try this exercise: Take two minutes to write down twenty things for which you are grateful. If you are struggling to think of twenty things, people, or places, then you probably need to practice more gratitude.

Begin with, "I am grateful because…" or, "I am thankful for…" It doesn't have to be a dissertation or short essay, just your way of seeing the best of things instead of bitter things. Keep a gratitude journal and list your activities and emotions. In my journal I wrote, "I am thankful for McDonald's fries, my cell phone that alerts me to important messages, and Visine because my eyes were itchy this morning." Another entry read, "I am grateful because it's winter and I can wear a hat and not have to do my hair every day, and that my boots cover my non-pedicured toes."

As you can tell from my journaling, a gratitude list doesn't always have to be serious or solemn. Now of course I'm thankful for health, family, and friends. I'm even thankful for the pains of life that have made me a stronger person, but you can also find gratitude in the most simple things of life. I learned a long time ago that the exercise of writing in a gratitude journal isn't so much about what you write, but how you feel when you're writing; the emotions that you experience as you are reflecting, imagining, and thinking about the things that you are grateful for. That's the real purpose. That's the gift of gratitude.

Melody Beattie said it well, "Gratitude turns what we have into enough and more. It turns denial into acceptance, chaos into order, confusion into clarity...it makes sense out of our past, brings peace for today, and creates a vision for tomorrow."

Smooth Sailing Biz Travel

Traveling with family is one thing, but when you're on the road with coworkers you may find that navigating those waters can either end with smooth sailing or sea sickness. To impress your boss and avoid a travel tsunami:

- **Keep the focus on work.** Make business a priority. You can socialize as long as you fulfill the purpose of your trip first, whether it's generating new business or attending educational events.

- **Take initiative** to make yourself indispensable to your boss. Volunteer to assist with a presentation, take minutes, or staff the company exhibit booth. Your efforts will pay off as you demonstrate your commitment to the success of the assignment.

- **Be courteous** when you may have to share hotel rooms or other accommodations with coworkers. Make the experience as pleasant as possible. Keep the bathroom tidy and hold down the noise if you're a night owl or early riser.

- **Don't lose sight of your purpose—remain professional.** And above all, project a professional image. Follow the same rules expected in the home office, including topics of conversation. This is not a time to let your guard down. It's a time to showcase who you are regardless of the setting.

Strive to be considerate and professional so you maintain good relations and advance your career.

Lead and Succeed

Teddy Roosevelt did it. Managers do it. And so, do I. If you want to be an outstanding leader, keep a leadership journal. Regardless of your position or power, leadership is about the goal—not the role. It's about making others better as a result of your presence and making sure that impact lasts in your absence.

Peter Drucker—an expert in the field of leadership and professional development said: "Follow effective action with quiet reflection. From the quiet reflection will come even more effective action." When you review your actions, it can reduce distractions.

To journal your way to success, just pick up your pen and begin. Journaling increases self-awareness—providing a clearer lens to recognize pitfalls and opportunities. The more you know—the more you can grow.

At the end of each day reflect on the way you handled a situation with a co-worker or loved one. Did you help or hurt the person? Did your actions influence steps forward or cause confusion? Were you able to learn, contribute in a positive way, or cause a delay? Detail your experiences to enhance your results.

Recalling your wins and challenges is a record of how you are progressing toward your goals and can assist to identify when you need to make changes so you can escape a disaster or excel your master plan.

Leaders are made not born. Live, learn, and lead to succeed!

PART II

STRESS BREAKERS

Burn it Up

If you sometimes feel that you are burning the candle at both ends when it comes to your job, or that your candle has just completely burned out, you are not alone. Polls reveal that burned-out employees outnumber the engaged employees 2 to 1. But you can reignite your energy for less stressful experiences!

New research suggests that there are at least three different types of burnout: overload, boredom, and wean out.

You may find yourself complaining, feeling as though those in control are limiting you from achieving your goals and ambitions—this is stress overload burnout. On the other hand, burnout that stems from boredom and lack of personal development is associated with an avoidance coping strategy. These people distance themselves from work and are more cynical. The final type of burnout is simply worn out. This coping strategy is based on giving up in the face of stress.

If you are overloaded, bored, or simply worn out, there are a few things you can do. Try emotion regulation: get control of your emotions and thoughts; don't react to the stress, instead learn to manage those emotions. Another tip is to increase cognitive flexibility: change what you are thinking about, how you are thinking about it, and even what you think about it. And last, ignite your inner capacity and infuse your life with awareness. Take charge of your life. Do something for yourself that no one else can do for you—by consciously and systematically working to defeat the stress, challenges, and demands of everyday life.

Don't give away your power and don't give up. Set goals and set your world on fire for greater success!

Pain, Pain Go Away

When times are tough, it's difficult to stay focused on your goals and aspirations. Dealing with painful and challenging circumstances limits your success—unless you begin to see your challenges as opportunities for growth.

You can experience more peace in these four ways:

1.   *Use your pain to drive you forward.* Pain is an indication that something, somewhere, isn't right. Is

your pain the result of unresolved issues? Confront your issues—don't run from them. The answer can lead to joy if you're willing to address the source of your discomfort.

2. *When you change your mindset, you change your outcomes.* You've heard the saying, "No pain, no gain." Recognize that life's challenges aren't meant to hurt you but to help you to grow. Positive thinking will help you successfully navigate through difficult times.

3. *Eliminate toxic habits.* Identify behaviors or interactions that are pain triggers. Whether it's a relationship, a specific person, or negative thinking, find ways to limit those situations and remove yourself from settings that stimulate pain and fear.

4. *Remember, you have a choice.* Decide today that you will not let those experiences own you. When you can manage the present, the future will take care of itself.

When the Going Gets Tough

Studies show that 85 percent of the things we worry about never happen. Yet stress is the most common reason for primary care visits with physicians. Americans spend billions of dollars on stress-related activities. Before you spend another dime or your time in the stress zone, try addressing and assessing to get your blessing:

- Ask and Act: *What is the most important thing I can do right now?* Sometimes the best thing we can do is nothing. Sometimes the best thing we can do is make a phone call. Focusing on and doing the best thing you can do in the midst of difficult times helps center you. It also increases your confidence in weathering each storm.

- Ask and Act: *What can I learn from the experience?* Extract a lesson from the stressing. There is a purpose for your pain. When things get hard, that's not always a sign that you're doing something wrong. It's often a sign that you're doing something right. You become the person you were meant to be through challenges.

- Ask and Act: *What are my choices?* Weigh the pros and cons. Creating a list of choices brings clarity to determining the best path forward. Then ask, **Will this matter five years from now?**

- Looking into the future and thinking about whether or not the difficulty will matter later in life often puts things into perspective.

Don't turn a molehill into mountain and imagine the worst possible outcome to every challenge. Have faith! What you are facing probably isn't as bad as you're imagining it to be.

When the going gets tough, start thinking, asking, and taking action to go beyond limitations to achieve success!

From Overwhelmed to In Control

Often when I ask someone how they are doing, they will respond, "Oh, I'm making it." At times, it can feel like we have way more stress than we can handle. Yet and still, we find a way to keep going. "Making it" is for the moment, but after a while, we may end up crashing. To stay in control and achieve more success to meet your objectives, try my six-step approach:

Step 1—Accept the situation. Stop right where you are and accept the situation for what it is.

Things will most likely get even worse if you keep going with the same thinking and actions! Stop and identify the reasons behind your downfall.

Step 2—Embrace your failures. This is the only way you'll be able to move on to resolving the situation.

Step 3—Avoid excuses. The last thing you want to do is blame the issue on something or somebody else. Sure, it's easy in stressful situations to refuse accountability. But just accept it for what it is, even if it means coming face to face with your shortcomings.

Step 4—Open up to others. Simply sharing can often help to ease some of the stress.

Step 5—Organize an approach. Now is your chance to change direction and pull yourself out of the rut and prevent the problem from happening again.

Step 6—Surround yourself with positive people. Use the strengths of trustworthy people to get you over the hump.

Being in over your head isn't a death sentence and shouldn't deter you from achieving your goals. In fact, *it's a perfect opportunity to be creative and begin again. It's your life... you're in control.*

From Worry to Winning

Are you a "What if" person? Always wondering what might happen if...? What if I lose my job? What if they say no? What if I get sick? What if I don't get married? What if the children don't listen? If that is you, you're not alone. About 18 percent of the US population suffers from anxiety disorders. In the age of information overload, when images of disaster are plastered all over our phones, televisions, computers, and phones, it's no wonder there is so much worry in the world.

"To further complicate matters, we are immune to the things that should give us the jitters. In reality, we are wired to pay attention to things that are scary," says Dr. Martin Rossman, author of *The Worry Solution*. "The number one function of the brain is to keep us alive, so we worry as a way to anticipate possible dangers and problem solve our way through them." Unfortunately, we've gotten so good at worrying, we don't always know how to shut it off.

But there are ways you can shut down worry and win. One way to do that is to focus only on what you can control. If you can't change it, affect it, or manage it, then why are you worrying? Focus your energy on the things you *can* change. It's often said that worry is like a rocking chair—you're moving, but you're not going anywhere.

Another way is to face the worry head-on—do this by imagining what is the worst thing that could possibly happen. Instead of avoiding the pain, uncertainty, and heartbreak, acknowledge those emotions. When you do, it takes the emotional power away. If you lose your job, you may worry, but you won't die. Many people have survived a job loss and many have landed in a better position.

Always remember, *the best of time is the rest of time.* Don't let worry get in your way of living a successful life today. Enjoy life! You only get one!

Wipe Out Worry

We don't need Webster, Wikipedia, or a Thesaurus to define worry. If asked, you'd probably reply that worry is a lack of faith, an anxious feeling, or the fear of failure or something negative happening. There's worry about employment, finances, a spouse, children, and the future. We worry about things we can't even control.

I encourage you to stop worrying. Here are a few tips to wipe out worry.

1. Acknowledge your fear or worry. Don't deny it exists. Talk to your worry—say something aloud like, "I'm afraid I could lose my job in this poor economy, but I'm going give 100 percent every day!" Or, "I'm worrying about my children but they belong to God and He won't fail."

2. Accept uncertainty. Remember that nothing in life is guaranteed. Worry serves you no good purpose. It is *not* an action—read that again— worry is *not* an action. Do whatever you need to do to *move on.* Call someone for encouragement. Take an exercise class. Scream like a crazy person. Get going!

3. Put it on paper. Sometimes we imagine the worst possible or unreasonable situations. When you write down your feelings, it's a lot easier to see whether they are even rational.

4. Pray. If you've prayed about it, then why are you worrying? Trust and believe that God's will will be done. The truth is, we spend time worrying about things that *never happen.*

Wipe out worry and make room for more creativity, innovation, and success.

Just Say, "NO"

Want more happiness, time, and energy in your days? Learn to say, "NO." Learning to say no can be one of the best things to happen in your life. It was for me. I used to accept all invitations. Why? I didn't want to disappoint the host. I used to take on extra assignments. Why? Because it had to get done...who else would do it. But I was "sick and tired" and everyone else seemed to be galloping through fields of tulips. That's when I took a step back and said NO.

Every "yes" adds another thing on your already-full plate and takes more energy away from you and your creativity. Just say NO if you:

- Take on too many commitments.

- Have too many ideas. Execute a few and put the rest in a folder labeled "Backburner."

- Suffer from information overload. Start blocking off downtime or focused worktime in your schedule. Here's how you can do that: Answer email at set times. Switch off your phone, or even leave it behind. The world won't end. I promise. (Unless you're my child and I'm calling you. But that's a Mommy thing.)

When you say yes to others, make sure you're not saying no to yourself. Learn to say no without explaining yourself or feeling guilty. No is a full sentence.

It's really simple. When you learn to say yes to yourself, you'll be able to say no to others with love. Say yes to more happiness, time, and energy in your life. The world won't end. I promise.

Eliminate to Elevate

Want know a secret to gain more time in your busy days? Read closely...the answer is *focus!* **Isn't it amazing how you are able to get twice as much done on the day before your vacation begins? More than likely you were able to pull it off because you were focused.**

Focusing our attention on what we should be doing versus what we are bombarded with can be a balancing act. The following are three ways to eliminate distractions:

- Eliminate doing something halfway. If you are working on a project, writing a report, or planning an event, complete it before moving on to another assignment. Focus and finish.

- Eliminate restarting. For example, if you started a new exercise program and see another promising better results, don't restart. Keep your current routine. Stopping and starting wastes time.

- Eliminate unnecessary tasks. Just because you've always done something a certain way doesn't mean it's the most efficient way. Organize and prioritize for better results.

Eliminate distractions and you will elevate your *success!*

Switch On

You missed a critical deadline at work, your child was suspended from school, the car broke down (again)…these are all examples of situations that could make us lose our minds. If you find yourself in a mental ditch, you to need to SWITCH. The SWITCH method will help you stay on course and to keep your cool.

S—Stop running in circles with your thinking and actions. Be still.

W—Wait. Make sure you allocate downtime to engage in activities that stimulate positivity.

I—Inhale and breathe. It clears your head and gives you an opportunity to balance the analytical processes of the mind with your emotions.

T—Think. Try to understand the root causes and interdependencies of the situation that you are in so you can address the issue.

C—Concentrate on your plan. Set clear goals that will get you the results you desire.

H—Have at it. Once you are clear about what you need to do, move on and execute.

SWITCH on your creativity. SWITCH on good thoughts. SWITCH on to de-stress and experience more success.

Hug it Out

During one of my coaching seminars to influence better employee engagement, I informed participants of the science behind hugging. Research shows that hugging (and also laughter) is extremely effective at improving and maintaining a healthy lifestyle. Then encouraged participants to hug more… hug your coworkers, hug your clients, hug your boss. Although they enjoyed the hug in the class session, most felt challenged to apply it in their workplace. I learned this technique from Jack Canfield and had a very similar experience.

Three weeks later, I received a note from one of the attendees. In part it read:

> I took on your challenge and began hugging more. One particular day I was in a crappy mood and wasn't feeling well when a coworker stopped by to ask me if I was giving out hugs…and although I was feeling despondent, I decided to make it a hugs day. Not only did it brighten their day it improved mine, and my headache actually disappeared.

Here's what I learned about hugging and shared with the group: Hugging is healthy. It helps the immune system, cures depression, reduce stress, and induces sleep. It's invigorating, rejuvenating and has no unpleasant side effects. It's nothing less than a miracle drug. Hugging is all natural. It's organic, naturally sweet, has no artificial ingredients, environmentally friendly and is 100 percent wholesome. Hugging is the ideal gift. Great for any occasion, fun to give and receive, shows you care, comes with its own wrapping paper and, of course, is fully returnable.

So, when in doubt, HUG it out.

De-stress to Be Your Best

Deadlines, job insecurity, and dealing with a difficult coworker or supervisor are just a few of the most common sources of stress in the workplace. If you're stressed out at work, you're not alone. In fact, according to the Attitudes in the American Workplace VII study:

- 82% of employees report that they feel some stress at work.

- 42% of workers say that the stress from their jobs affects their personal relationships.

- 35% of those surveyed believe that workplace stress harms their physical and emotional health.

But there is good news. Regardless of the source of stress at your workplace, there are steps that you can take to defeat stress and feel more calm, centered, and in control when you are at work.

Mix things up. If you're feeling frustrated with a difficult or time consuming task, switch gears. Gain a new perspective on an old or complex issue by working on something else for a while. When you change tasks, your mind is forced to think differently, which is often the wellspring to finding creative solutions and renewed energy. In addition to clearing your mind, switching tasks helps your body to lower your heart rate and stress-related hormone levels.

Take a mini mental vacation. If you are feeling overwhelmed, tense, and stressed out from situations at work that you can't control, like dealing with angry customer or demanding manager, close your eyes for a few moments and concentrate on your breathing. Clear your mind with slow, deliberate breaths. As you focus on your breathing, loosen your muscles as you inhale exhale. And repeat positive affirmations to yourself like, "I feel calm, centered, and ready to face any challenges."

Even if you enjoy your job, work stress can still be a regular occurrence. Act now so you can de-stress and be your best!

Don't Stress About It

One of the barriers to living successfully is living with stress. Some people say, "Get used to it," or "It's part of life." In coaching, we recognize that stress *does not* have to be part of your life. There are things you can do to reduce the stress so you can be your best. The following are three simple examples:

1. Take time to plan and prioritize. Would you believe a very common source of stress is a *to-do list?* It's true! At one point in my life, my to-do list became a torture list. It seemed the words were jumping off the paper, taunting and teasing me, "You'll never get this done." I know I heard it. I used to write things down that weren't on the list so I could cross them off just to feel like I accomplished something. It's a sad truth. I

was a victim of the to-do list. But I can declare that I've overcome. If you face this same challenge, try this, instead of obsessing about the list, identify one task that would move you closer to your highest goal and do that task first. The rest is bonus!

2. Assume people have good intentions. Since you can't read minds, you don't really know the "why" behind the "what" that people do. I used to think that people were talking about me if they stopped talking when I walked into the room. It would cause me so much anxiety. Then one day a friend said, "Girl, ain't nobody thinking about you!" After several minutes of knee-slapping, I realized she was probably right. And I resolved that even if I thought people were talking about me, it's better to assume they had good intentions.

3. Reduce the chatter. To think clearly and mentally regroup, it's important to get in a space with little noise or distraction. Remember day dreaming? Staring out the window, looking at the sky and smiling? That was a way of purifying your thoughts. Spend a few minutes each day thinking nothing but good thoughts.

Remember, stressing won't lead you any quicker to a better life. Continue to practice ways to improve your habits and thoughts for greater success!

Why Worry?

It's often reported that 85 percent of the things we worry about never happen. The earliest source related to that reality is said to be Thomas S. Kepler, a respected biblical scholar. Kepler wrote about a woman who realized fears were ruining her life. She began to keep track of what was worrying her and she found:

- 40% of the things she worried about were about things that would never happen.

- 30% of the things she worried about already happened, water under the bridge.

- 12% of the things she worried about were others' opinions; and when she thought about it, she realized that criticisms are often made by those who are jealous or insecure, and therefore unjust criticism is a disguised compliment.

- 10% of the things she worried about were needless health worries, which made her health worse as she worried.

- 8% of the things she worried about were "legitimate," since life has some real problems to meet.

If you consider those statistics, it would seem that only 8 percent of the things that we worry about are worth the worry. That's proof enough to stop worrying about what could go wrong and get excited about what could go right.

Life is like a camera: focus on what's important, capture the good times, develop from the negatives, and if things don't work out…take another shot.

Too Blessed to Be Stressed

Stress kills! There have been numerous studies that link stress to cancer, heart attacks, high blood pressure and depression. But a study by Harvard University shines a new light on the effects of stress. Researchers have proven that it is not the stress that kills but the BELIEF that stress kills that is the real culprit. In fact, they deducted that more people die from the belief that stress was harmful to their health than those who died from skin cancer, HIV, and homicide. Now that's a WOW revelation.

This means that how you think about stress matters. If you change your mind about stress, you can change your body's response to stress. Think about it this way, when you're stressed, your heart rate goes up and blood vessels constrict. Instead of thinking of it as a harmful experience, think of the reaction as your body helping you to rise to the occasion. Studies show that people who viewed stress that way stayed relaxed and their heart muscles looked the same as when they experienced moments of joy.

Who knew you could be blessed by stress. During times when you feel overwhelmed, say these things to keep stress in its place:

- Stress is my friend.

- Stress is harmful only if I believe it is.

- I'm too blessed to be stressed.

Then let go of the stress and focus your energy on things you can impact for better results.

Time to Make a Change

The mini-storage business is flourishing due to the excess in our lives. We are overburdened and overwhelmed with too much clutter, too many papers, worn-out clothes, or broken and unneeded items. When you clear out the old, you can make room for the new.

If your clothes closet is so full that you struggle to find something to wear every day, you've got an excess mess. If there is anything new you want in your life, you've got to make room for it—psychologically and physically. Make a commitment to dump, complete, or delegate things so you can move on and bring new activity, abundance, relationships, and excitement into your life.

Here's a simple plan to make a change today:

1. Make a list.

2. Choose three items to work on.

3. Set a date to get it done.

4. Get started.

What's on your list? Promises not kept, acknowledged, or renegotiated? Closets overflowing with clothes that don't fit, are out-of-fashion, or worn-out? Junk drawers full of useless items? People you need to forgive?

Do something today that your future will thank you for, because tomorrow is too late, yesterday is over, and *now* is exactly the right moment to *start!* Don't drag excess into another day. You can do it! Believe it and achieve it!

Stress Immunity

You might think that boosting your immune system is all about taking vitamin pills and watching your blood pressure. The truth is, protecting yourself from illness depends on your mind as much as your body. In fact, there's a growing field of science called psychoneuroimmunology that's devoted to how your personality and mood affect your immune system.

Here are the facts:

Chronic stress may be responsible for as much as 90 percent of all doctor visits in the US, according to the Centers for Disease Control and Prevention. When stress hormones like cortisol remain present for too long, they can cause disruptions that lead to premature aging, heart conditions, and other issues. So what can you do?

- **Slow down.** Take a deep breath when you find yourself rushing around. Stretch out and release the tension.

- **Trim your to-do list.** Look for items that you can scratch off your agenda. Maybe do laundry only once a week.

- **Rest and relax.** Go to bed and rise at the same time each day. Set a sleeping routine. And when you need a break, listen to your body, take a walk, meditate, or pray.

Recognizing the mind-body connection may help you catch fewer colds and lower your risk for more serious illnesses. So the next time you feel stressed, instead of continuing to plow through, digging a deeper stress hole won't do. Take the time to clear your mind and reset your thoughts to better manage your stress so you can be your best. The truth is, worrying doesn't change the outcomes, but less worry can help you live a longer and healthier life.

PMS

On an early morning drive, I noticed a police officer had pulled a car over to the side of the road, and like a true rubber-necker, as I was passing I looked to see who was in the car. I saw a female driver staring ahead, while three young children were reaching over the seats trying to hit one another. She looked exhausted. I thought, *Wow, she's got to be stressed*. I began thinking about how her morning must have been. Getting up early to fix breakfast before waking the children, screaming up the stairs for them to hurry, climbing back up the stairs because they're wrestling instead of getting dressed. One can't find a shoe, now she's on a hunt. Finally she's chasing the kids out the door, loading them in the car...then oops, one forgot the lunch bag...wait! That's my story!

I would assume that is also the story of many others. We are constantly juggling home, family, work, and friendships which can at times be stressful. During a Professional Women's Association meeting, Star Jones, the former host of the television program, *The View*, and President of the organization presented a message of encouragement. After having open heart surgery, she discussed how she was forced to make changes in her life. Managing stress was one of the things she had to do better. Her system of managing stress is called PMS. But it's not what you are probably thinking.

P stands for Physical strength. Adapt a wellness regime that includes healthy nourishment, exercise, and regular physician visits.

M is for Mental health. Do what makes you happy. Star loves to cook and she listens to messages and songs of inspiration.

S is for Support system. Surround yourself with people you love and those who care for your well-being.

Managing stress is all about taking charge of your thoughts, emotions, health, and the way you deal with problems. Find your own version of PMS to live a healthier, happier, successful life.

Face the FACTS

The *fact* is, everyone is seeking happiness in life! If you want more happiness, the following are the FACTS:

F—Forgive others. It's often said that forgiveness is the gift you give to yourself. The people you are holding hostage in your mind don't even know they're in prison. The only person in captivity is you. Free yourself by letting go of the thoughts that are holding *you* back.

A—Accept your mistakes. We *all* make mistakes. If you're not making mistakes, you're not trying hard enough. Keep growing and keep going!

C—Cry; big girls and boys *do* cry. When you cry, the body moves from a state of high arousal or stress to one more associated with relaxation. Breathing and heart rate slows, sweating decreases, and you're more relaxed after you've cried. So cry it out and move on.

T—Thank God for everything. Thank Him for waking you, breaking you, making you, and keeping you. Gratitude is a powerful generator of happiness.

S—Smile always. Smiling has been shown to increase productivity while performing tasks. There's real truth to the "Whistle while you work" mentality. When you're able to accomplish more, you feel better.

Find joy in the *fact* that you were created from excellence for excellence!

Be Still

Contrary to popular belief, being productive does not always mean doing more. In fact, one vital aspect that many people forget is that we also need *stillness.*

Every day we get caught up in a whirlwind of choices and activities: what to have for breakfast, watch TV or listen to the radio, what shoes to wear (oh, that's a female thing). What happens is that our brains fill up. We get distracted. And even if we don't, life has a habit of, well, happening!

So, we *must* make time to clear our minds so we can see what is most important. We see what we can let go of, what to delegate, what we need to change, what we can say no to—and what we need to say yes to. Stillness allows us to adapt our plans and actions to the reality of what actually happens in our lives.

How can you pause and find stillness? It's easy and takes just a couple minutes. First, stop rushing from one thing to the next. Take the opportunity to pause *between* your tasks and appointments. *Pause during breaks* in your day, before you start work, at lunch, and at the end of the work day. Just *pause* for no good reason! And don't fill every spare minute with Face-book, email, or by starting the next task. Instead, sit still and breathe. Stare out the window. Let the dust settle and wait for your mind to clear.

Jean Blomquist wrote, *"Wisdom means listening to the still, small voice, the whisper that can be easily lost in the whirlwind of busyness, expectations, and conventions of the world."* And Don-nie McClurkin reminds us of what to do when we've done all we can—JUST STAND. Become more productive by being still. It *can* change your life!

PART III

RELATIONSHIPS

Teamwork

A key component to living successfully—meaning living with faith, hope, joy, and love—is *teamwork*. If you ask successful people how they "made it," they always talk about people who helped them on the journey. It takes a village to raise a child and it takes a team for *life success*. You need a team for work, when your boss is acting crazy; for family, when the kids are acting up; for business, when the numbers aren't adding up; and for spiritual support, when the negative energy is heavy.

The following is a list of individuals who should be on your team:

Captain—the one who has been there and done that; they mentor you and help you navigate through and around both opportunities and landmines.

Rookies—someone you can pour into and share experiences and learnings. You will grow as you help them.

Trainer—someone who supports you because the trainer knows people, events, and information you need to stay competitive.

Coach—someone who helps you build a plan, encourages and motivates you, and provides accountability so you stick with the plan to achieve your goals.

In the game of life, build a strong team of supporters. You'll score the winning baskets, hit the home runs, make touchdowns, and be a champion every time.

The True You

Too often I hear stories where individuals are unhappy or they lack fulfillment because of their desire to have more purposeful and meaningful relationships—but they keep attracting the wrong type people into their lives.

So how do you attract the right people into your life? This may shock you, but you must be yourself. Be you! **The privilege of a lifetime is to become who you are truly are.** If the wrong people are showing up in your life time and time again, on some level, you're putting out an *inauthentic version of yourself.*

- Do you smile and nod when you really want to give someone a piece of your mind?

- Do you neglect to mention the things that you really love or care about for fear that you'll be judged or criticized?

- Do you have a work mode, friend mode, and family mode?

Answering yes to any of those questions is an indication that you're likely not being true to you, which provides an inaccurate perception of who you are, thereby creating opportunities for the wrong people to settle into your life.

Let the real you stand up! Order the meal that you really want, talk about the things that light you up and speak your truth. Start small and be prepared to let the wrong people fall out of your life—so the right people can step in. As Shakespeare said, "To thine own self be true!"

It's Not about You

It's official! According to the American Institute of Stress, numerous studies show that job stress is far and away the major source of stress for American adults, and it has escalated progressively over the past few decades.

Although it may be challenging, you can build support and rapport in the workplace and put good energy in the atmosphere. If you want to make a positive impact in your workplace, implement these actions in your daily routine:

- **Acknowledge your coworkers.** Start by letting those in the other cubicles know that you see them as human beings. Wish everyone a cheerful "Good morning!"

- **Show interest.** Ask the receptionist how her son's soccer game went. Welcome others back from vacation or sick leave.

- **Listen actively.** Listening is an effective way to show you care. Give your full attention to your coworkers instead of rehearsing what you're going to say next. Clarify what others are saying and offer thoughtful comments.

- **Pay compliments.** Praise others for their talents and accomplishments. Encourage them to talk about their victories.

- **Let go of expectations.** You probably have coworkers who will remember your birthday, but occasionally make comments that seem to undermine you. *Accept both the strengths and weaknesses of your coworkers.* Focus on treating others well, and consider it a bonus if they reciprocate.

Work is about personal relationships as well as tasks. Creating a supportive workplace may be the most important part of your job. Make it a priority! You and your colleagues will achieve more and feel less stressed along the way.

The Awe of Envy

Do you get a disturbing feeling when a colleague receives the promotion you wanted? Or when your best friend is planning her wedding while you're not even in a steady relationship with anyone?

An envious attitude may seem unpleasant, but it can also have an upside. If you tap into the positivity of the emotion, envy can provide insights you can use to understand yourself better and enhance your relationships. Here's how you can prevent and manage those nagging resentments:

- **Acknowledge your envy** instead of trying to cover it up. Open up. This will loosen its hold on you.

- **Ask for advice.** Forget about beating your competition. You'll have more to show for your efforts if you concentrate on learning from them. If a friend launches a new business, invite your friend out to lunch to pick up some pointers.

- **Examine your relationships.** Are you living vicariously through your friends? Coveting your friends' exotic travels or their resilience in taking adult education courses could reveal what you really want to be doing. Pursue your own dreams with a plan that fits your budget and schedule. It's more satisfying to take action than sit on the sidelines.

- **Adjust your attitude.** If you feel life is unfair and you deserve the good fortune that others experience, adjust your attitude. It will make you more buoyant and content. Some events are beyond your control, but you can decide how you respond to them.

Stop envy from turning you into a green-eyed monster. Head off resentments before they begin, and channel any and all competitive feelings in a positive direction.

Trust or Bust!

Most people have been deceived, mistreated, or taken advantage of by another person at some point in our lives. Some have an easy time recovering from these situations, while others find it challenging to trust again. And taken too far, it's easy to become socially isolated without trust.

As humans, we are social creatures who require interactions with others in order to be at our best. Try these techniques to trust again and move forward in your relationships:

- **Find the source.** No one is born untrusting. Something has happened to cause distrust to become your *modus operandi* when dealing with others. It may be several situations from your past.

- **Keep the past in the past.** Did your ex cheat on you five years ago? That's one person, a single instance, and five years ago. *Hanging on to old hurts prolongs suffering.* Let go and move on.

- **Learn.** If you believe someone burned you in the past, learn ways to avoid a similar situation down the road.

- **Go slowly.** Some people trust way too much or way too little. *Often, the best solutions are found near the middle.* Allow people to earn your trust.

Trust is a must in order for any relationship to be successful. Use these solutions to let go and grow!

The Power of Praise

If you want to be encouraged, encourage someone else. Each time you give praise, you not only uplift the other person, but your spirits are positively awakened and that can lead to a more positive outlook on life. Give praise generously by:

- **Accentuating the positive.** Be genuine with praise by mentioning specific acts or characteristics that you admire about others. If someone was expedient in delivering an assignment, make sure to mention the specific assignment and use encouraging terms that demonstrate your thoughtfulness and recognizes their accomplishment. This is a favorite tactic I use with my children, even though they are adults. It also conveys how much I appreciate them.

- **Creating a friendly environment.** It's easier for people to take risks and grow if they feel supported. Commending others can help them relax and feel less anxious.

- **Focusing on effort as well as ability.** Studies show acknowledging people for their perseverance and hard work makes them feel more comfortable taking on new challenges.

Your praise has power! Success isn't just about accomplishment, it's also about how the things you do in your life motivate and inspire others to do something motivating and inspiring in theirs.

Motivate and Elevate

Have you ever asked your children to pick up after themselves and then you hear moans and groans as a response? Or maybe you've asked a coworker or employee for support on a project and they reluctantly participate in meetings and project updates? Whether spouses, kids, team members, or employees, it takes leadership abilities to get people motivated so you don't have to nag them.

To gain the results you are seeking:

- **Stop bribing them**. Rewards definitely work, but they just motivate people to get rewards. When the rewards go away, people stop working. And if you want anything other than basic effort, rewards can actually backfire.

- **Inspire them emotionally.** People take action when they are inspired emotionally to be engaged. Just as we respond to revenge, jealousy, or fear, positive emotions are powerful motivators. In fact, individuals rarely do anything they don't feel, and it's very hard to resist things we do feel. You can change behavior by addressing their feelings. Ask, "How do you feel about this amazing new opportunity to showcase your talents?" Listen and support them.

- **Emphasize progress.** Harvard researchers found that of all the positive events that influence inner work life, the single most powerful is ***progress in meaningful work.*** Encourage people to reflect on how far they've come and the good work they've done. Have them share an accomplishment to get started or reboot.

Now that you've got people on board, keep the motivation flowing by creating unity. Get them excited around the cause. Share a story or belief so they connect with one another. People are engaged and motivated by *why* they do things more than *what* they do.

Set an example through your own motivation. ***Be the power and others will follow.***

Show Them What You're Saying

You are a hardworking, serious, motivated person—but is your body language communicating the same message? First impressions are important. Use your body language to your advantage. Try these three quick ways to better engage and project a positive image:

1. *Move with good posture.* Walk and stand tall, head up and shoulders back. Fight the habit to walk and look toward the ground. Instead, walk with your chin up looking forward. Standing up straight is the number one way to communicate confidence and self-assurance.

2. *Make direct eye contact.* Not looking someone directly in the eye can speak volumes. Shifty or downcast eyes can make you appear shy, disinterested, rude, or nervous. On the flip side,

connecting with someone eye to eye makes the other person feel that you are interested in them and what they have to say.

3. *Control your hands.* Have you ever talked with someone and their hands are moving as if they are conducting an orchestra? That is very distracting. Refrain from habits like drumming on the table, clicking a pen, or messing with your hair. You want the person you're talking with to concentrate on what you are *saying,* not what you're *doing.* Controlling your hands will help you appear relaxed and focused.

Let people *see* what you're *saying.* Stand tall, make eye contact, and control your hands so you can shake more hands and make connections for more success.

Rapport

Being likeable is a highly desirable trait. In fact, to have a successful career, relationships with our coworkers are dependent on the ability to gain influence and trust.

To cultivate harmonious relationships with coworkers and managers and enable an atmosphere where you can grow professionally and increase your productivity requires that you build rapport to be adored. The following are three recommendations to enjoy more fruitful workplace relationships:

- *People enjoy talking about themselves.* When engaging in small groups, find out what they enjoy doing. Ask questions like what's your favorite restaurant or movie. That will get the conversation going. Listen with enthusiasm and chime in. Try not to zone out or have a disinterested look on your face as they are answering. Instead, lean forward a little bit and nod your head occasionally to let them know you're connecting with them and are interested.

- *Everybody loves a sense of humor.* You don't have to be "on" the whole time you're talking with someone. However, if you can make an occasional joke or share a funny story, this will help create rapport. To be safe, make a joke about yourself or the situation you're in. Avoid making critical comments of others in an attempt at humor. This could backfire and have the opposite effect.

- *Avoid seeming too needy.* Some individuals come on too strongly. If you try too hard and overdo it, you can actually push others away rather than establish rapport. Give genuine compliments and create an aura that illuminates an approachable and honest spirit.

Successfully implementing these recommendations will help you stand out and develop relationships that will be beneficial for your career. Becoming a better person is a daily journey. Keep growing!

People Passion

My grandmother used to say, "Some folks bring joy wherever they go; others bring joy *when* they go." Every person carries an energy. Some energy is positive and some can be harmful. Other's presence in our lives affects our health and passion pursuit.

In Gordon MacDonald's book *Renewing Your Spiritual Passion,* he discusses five kinds of people who affect our well-being:

1. **Passion Igniters.** These people are very resourceful. We gain energy from their courage and maturity. They make us feel uplifted and inspired. And we lean on them for direction.

2. **Passion Partners.** These are people who you are bound to for a purpose, and together you stimulate one other for better outcomes.

3. **Passion Followers.** These are very trainable people. By sharing ourselves, we stir our own passion to serve and grow because of the effect it has on them.

4. **Passion Pleasers.** Are there people in your life who clap, laugh, and build your ego? That's pleasant, however, they contribute very little to our passion. They don't add or subtract from it. They simply enjoy it.

5. **Passion Zappers.** These people are very draining and suck away our energy.

To maintain a healthy passion for success, understand people passion and those who bring the energy we need to develop. Everyone is in your life for a reason—know what it is for your growth and happiness.

Listen Up

Communication involves two things: Speaking and listening. Unfortunately, we don't always master the listening part. There is an art to *listening*. Studies show eighty-five percent of our success in learning from other people is based on how well we listen. In other words, our success or failure with communication can be determined before we even say anything.

Listening is active and powerful, not a passive activity. Try these three action steps to become a better listener:

- **Think before you speak.** What do most of us do when we're upset? We talk. When we're confused, surprised, shocked? Talk. However, listening is a two-part process. During one part, we listen. During the other, we speak. What we say is proof of how well we've listened.

- **Listen with respect.** To learn from people, you have to listen to them with respect. This means engaging the speaker with your eye contact and body language, showing that you are interested in what they are saying, so that you can keep learning from what they are saying.

- **Ask yourself,** *Is it worth it?* Listening requires answering this question before you even speak. Instead of thinking, *What's in it for me?*, take it a step further and ask, *What's in it for them?*

Listening is simple but it's not always easy. Engage by asking questions that show you're paying attention, move the conversation forward, and require the other person to talk. Keep practicing and you will reap amazing benefits!

Engage and Expand

You often hear, "It's not what you know, it's *who* you know that matters." Networking helps to connect you with mentors, customers, clients, colleagues, and people of influence. But, it can become costly to build these connections. Try these following tips to network without busting the budget.

- **Volunteer at events**. You'll have to work, but you won't have to pay to get in. This gives you a chance to meet the event organizers and other volunteers, in addition to attendees. You'll also make a great impression because of your servitude.

- **Create an online community.** Use social media. Lead discussions that will build your reputation, and others will share your content, further extending your reach.

- **Connect virtually.** Schedule face to face meetings online versus in a coffee shop or café. It will have the same impact and you'll eliminate the time and costs of travelling.

- **Network using your network.** Your current connections probably know people you're interested in meeting. A former coaching client who owned a catering business received three bookings in her first month of operation by inviting friends and family to a tasting, and asking them to bring guests.

- **Make networking a habit.** Look for opportunities to connect with the people you come across every day. Try engaging in discussion with someone at the salon, barber shop, or coffee cafe. It may feel awkward at first and you won't be successful every time, but you'll get better at recognizing potential connections and more skillful with conversation starters. It's not always who you know. It's who knows you.

Use these tips to build influential relationships and expand your brand for greater success.

Care and Share

One of the most requested training programs I present is on the topic of workplace conflict. I am alarmed by the number of people in the workplace who admit (some without a hint of regret) that they just "don't care" about many of the people they work with.

Without question, the endless pressures of today's workplace, exacerbated by technological and economic disruptions, are taking their toll on workers. Many people are experiencing *emotional fatigue,* with few outlets for expression, especially in the workplace, and that leads to workplace conflict.

But the bottom line is, people need people. A Gallup study of workplace attitudes surveyed eight million people. Those who felt that *"My supervisor, or someone at work, seems to care"* were more productive and have more engaged customers. So what's the problem that hinders relationships in the workplace? There are several problems:

- **The objectification of others.** People are not things. They are not tasks or means to an end.

Individuals who think of people as objects have a much harder time developing successful workplace relationships. Since a majority of our communication is conveyed nonverbally, what you are thinking will come across in your body language or behaviors, making it difficult to forge bonds with others.

- **Results-only thinking.** If you say, "I don't care, anything goes to get things done. They'll get over it. Nothing gets in the way of my goals," this type of thinking might apply to you. While it's great to be focused on outcomes, they are often achieved at the expense of relationships.

- **Lack of trust among teams and individuals.** To gain more trust, become aware of how others perceive you and keep your promises when it comes to meeting deadlines, supporting your coworkers, and being timely.

Cultivating effective workplace relationships takes skill and commitment. Show you care by choosing to have an inviting attitude. Greet people warmly. Share more about who you are, your values, and the things that are important to you. Let your light shine and brighten the pathway for others.

A Good Samaritan

Any parent will tell you that getting young children to behave while out to dinner is no easy task. And when you're a single mom with three kids, that task can be very challenging. Still, that's exactly what one North Carolina mom has done every Friday for the last few years, despite several moves and a messy divorce.

ABC News reported that while at a local Pizza Hut, a divorced mom approached a man sitting in a nearby booth and apologized in advance for the noise she knew her three young children were likely to make. The man said no problem.

It wasn't until after the man left that his kindness was revealed: before leaving the restaurant, he paid for their meal, purchased a gift card for them, and left the mom a note that read: "I don't know your back story, but I have had the privilege of watching you parent your children for the past thirty minutes. I have watched you teach your children about the importance of respect, education, proper manners, communication, self-control, and kindness—all while being very patient. I will never cross your path again, but am positive that you and your children have amazing futures. Keep up the good work and when it starts to get tough, don't forget that others may be watching and will need the encouragement of seeing a good family being raised."

The mom remarked, "I've had the worst few years of my life and I never get recognition like this. You never know who's watching you."

We know that God hears and sees all. He knows what you are going through. And when you think you're at the end of your rope, He will dispatch an angel to encourage you. Be an angel today. Someone is watching you.

Reverse the Critical Curse

We all have our own set of values. While having values is very positive, there's also a risk of getting over-enthusiastic and expecting others to behave a certain way. It's important to realize that there's no single way to live life or view the world. You're limiting your personal growth and enjoyment when you expect others to live according to your rules and do things the way you would.

I've been guilty of this a time or two. Like when my granddaughter was born and I interjected my thoughts consistently on how she should be raised, how much sleep she needed... you know what I mean. This often led to my daughter rolling her eyes or whispering underneath her breath. Then I remembered how I felt as a first-time mother. I then recognized that I could make my life and visits with my granddaughter much more enjoyable when I accepted my daughter's style of parenting.

If this sounds familiar, you can remove your expectations and be less critical by becoming more open-minded. This can be accomplished by monitoring your thoughts. Practice positive thoughts and ways to encourage versus discourage.

Another strategy to be less critical is to pause and take a deep breath. How many times have you wished you could take back something you've said? By pausing, you interrupt your thought pattern and give yourself time to think before you say something you might regret.

A final way to be less critical is to understand that people, including yourself, are doing the best they can. That's not to say that everyone is living up to their potential. But everyone has their own past, tragedies, upbringing, issues, and way of viewing the world. The person you're judging might be doing a lot better than you think if only you knew the entire story.

Don't criticize...strategize; you'll get more out of life if you reverse the critical curse through your thinking, words, and actions.

Sorry

Have you wronged someone else, and now you wish to make it right? Apologies can be awkward and uncomfortable, but a good apology communicates a willingness to admit your mistakes and be a better person. It also shows that you value the relationship and want to ensure that there are no hard feelings between you and the offended person.

Even if you don't feel like the situation was your fault, asking forgiveness for your part in the argument may be the quickest way to smooth things over and save your relationship. A well-delivered apology can soothe hurt feelings and draw others closer to you. So, how can you express regret in a way that benefits you?

Just saying you're sorry may be enough if it's sincere. Find the right words to express a willingness to accept your part of the blame. Some phrases to use include:

- I'm sorry.
- I apologize.
- Please forgive me.
- I know I've wronged you.
- I hate that this has come between us.
- What can I do to make things right?
- Can we talk out our differences?
- Please let me explain.

If you open the conversation this way, you demonstrate that you truly want to make things better.

Keep in mind, *I'm sorry* is a statement. *I won't do it again* is a promise. *How do I make it up to you* is a responsibility.

R_E_S_P_E_C_T

Respect makes our relationships run more smoothly. Feeling appreciated puts us at ease and helps us bond more closely. We share a sincere regard for each other. We know that our welfare matters, and we treat each other with courtesy and fairness.

The more respect you give, the more you're likely to receive in return. But what if that doesn't happen? Here are my top five suggestions to help you gain more respect from others and feel more valued.

- **Honor your commitments.** Keep your word. It's better to under-promise and over-deliver than the opposite.

- **Think before speaking.** Do your research before you comment on a subject. Ask yourself if you're adding anything valuable to a discussion. Imagine how you would feel if you were on the receiving end of your own feedback and choose your words accordingly.

- **Communicate directly.** Being straightforward sometimes requires courage, but the rewards are worth it. Ask for what you need and extend the same opportunity to others.

- **Learn to say no.** Turn down requests graciously if you believe they are unreasonable or you have other commitments. Making the best use of your time is smart, not selfish.

- **Decline being taken for granted.** If your generosity seems wasted, you may be right. Be selective about how you give away your time, money, and other resources. Support charities that welcome your offer to volunteer. Exchange hospitality with friends who invite you back.

RESPECT is not imposed nor begged for—it's earned and offered.

Pass it On

Every morning my husband is faithful in going to the gym to exercise. It's his daily routine. Something special happened one morning that he shared with me. When he was at the gym, a man approached and said to him, "Sir, I want to give you something. I see you here every morning and you always have a big smile." The man gave him a card that read, "Thank you so much! That smile you shared brightened my day. The world needs more smiles, so pass this little card on to the next great smiler you meet."

We all like giving and receiving gifts, and many of the best gifts in life are free. Here are a few other gifts you can share with others:

- **Encouragement.** The word "encourage" means "to give courage, confidence, or hope," and it has been called the most important ingredient in building positive personal and professional relationships.

- **Laughter.** You can change a mood from drab to fab in an instant with a good joke or great story. It's one of the best mental cures for any dull or despondent disposition.

- **Support.** You can donate your time to a cause you believe in, or visit a sick friend or relative or support someone who is pursuing their dream with your ideas or talents.

Continue to seek the good and the good will find you. If you give, it will come back to you.

When Haters Bait

A friend was really excited about the remarkable progress she was making on her weight loss journey when someone remarked that she shouldn't get too excited because she had a long way to go. The person added, "Many people fail anyway, so don't be surprised if you have don't reach your goals." As she shared the story with me, I thought, *how unfortunate… sometimes the more significant your accomplishments, the more criticism you may face.*

Here's the truth: criticism is part of life. If you learn to deal with it, not only will your life be less stressful, it'll be easier to be successful.

When haters try to bait you:

- **Take a deep breath** or count to 10. Seriously! Get as calm as you can before you respond to criticism. Calmness enables more intelligent thinking that can prevent you from reacting in a way that may do more harm than good.

- **Thank the person.** This is the best way to disarm your critics. "Thank you for thinking about me." "Thank you for being concerned about my situation." Then…

- **Move on.** Regardless whether the criticism was accurate or not, just move on. Focus on your next task; avoid wasting time looking backward. And…

- **Reward yourself.** Each time you receive criticism and handle it appropriately, take the time to congratulate yourself. Be proud that you had so much control over yourself and were even possibly able to gain something positive from the experience.

In all, *don't let compliments get to your head. And don't let criticism get to your heart.*

Family Matters

My little sister came to visit from Europe which was a wonderful surprise. My brother-in-law had been in the United States Army for eighteen years. Most of the relationship had been limited to phone conversation versus visits to each other's home. It can be tough keeping family together over such distances, but that is even more reason to maintain those bonds and closeness.

If your family life is falling apart, start the rebuilding process with these simple strategies:

- **Schedule a weekly conference call.** Treat the call like any other essential meeting. Once it's scheduled, only unforeseen emergencies can postpone them. Ask questions and show genuine interest. You'll feel the warmth and love of family during and after the call ends.

- **Make a big deal out of birthdays.** Make a special effort each year to treasure those special days. Send a real birthday card via snail mail. And write some good wishes so they see how much they mean to you.

- **Resolve issues in a family setting.** If there's an issue with one of your siblings, bring everyone on board, which helps to make discussions impartial. Having loved ones supporting you will steer things in the direction of resolution versus chaos.

- **Make family decisions together.** Regardless of how far apart you are, remember that everybody's input is important.

Your family is your army. The members are to protect, defend, and love each other. LIVE! LOVE! And make family relationships LAST!

Forgive and Live

Everyone has suffered some sort of emotional hurt through the words or actions of another. Experiencing hurt feelings is completely natural, but sometimes the hurt lasts longer than it needs to which makes it harder to be happy and, if we can't let go and move on, it can ruin relationships.

Forgiveness is one of the ways you can profoundly change your life. It's not always easy, but it's a skill that can be learned with practice.

To move forward in forgiveness...

- **Think about all the advantages of letting go of your hurt.** Make a list of what you would gain by forgiving what has happened to you. Think about how free you will feel. How your relationship with that person could change.

- **Then list the disadvantages.** What toll is it taking on you and the people around you? Is holding on to the negative feelings going to solve anything?

- **You'll realize the answer is to let go.** Let's face it, most people don't miraculously lose 25 pounds or start saving an extra $100 every month. Anything positive normally starts with an intention. So commit to finding a way to forgive and move on.

You have a choice about how you interpret things and the actions you take afterward. When you choose to forgive, you'll immediately feel better. We're at our best when we act with compassion.

There's a saying: refusing to forgive is like drinking poison and waiting for the other person to die. LIVE fully. Forgiving someone may cost you your pride, but not forgiving them can cost you your freedom.

Your Circle

When coaching clients, I often hear that they are struggling to manage relationships with those in their circle while pursuing their dreams or just living peacefully day to day. Let's face it, we are a limited resource. You can't be all things to all people. During a broadcast, T.D. Jakes discussed ways to identify and categorize the people in your circle. There are three types: confidants, constituents, and comrades.

Confidants are intelligent, motivating, and trustworthy. This is your ride or die crew—you can depend on them. Confidants are only a very few individuals, like a spouse, childhood friend, or business partner.

Constituents are part of your life because you share similar goals. They are only interested in your destination because you're going in the same direction. However, if they find someone else who will get them there faster, they will leave you. You cannot depend on them.

The last group are *comrades.* They are part of your life because they are against what you are against. They will fight with you against a common cause—like cures for cancer or to get a particular political candidate in office—but as soon as the battle is over, they will leave you because they don't need you anymore.[1]

It's important to identify the role people play in your personal and professional life because it determines with whom you spend your time—as well as your level of productivity and accomplishment. You are the company you keep. Ask yourself, *Who am I hanging out with? What are they doing for me? What do they have me thinking?* Then ask yourself if that's ok. Things don't get better by chance only—they get better by choice and change. Figure out who's in your circle to improve your relationships and productivity.

Friends to the End

Do you have friends who just won't bend and they're sucking the life out of you? They expect you to be at their beck and call and get upset if you tell them they are wrong? You love them, but it feels like they demand too much? Trying to be supportive of your friends is beneficial for them, but it could be hazardous to your own peace of mind.

To build healthier and happier relationships, set limits. Let your friends know the boundaries you require to feel comfortable. You may decide that you can take only one call a day, barring any emergencies. Maybe you're unavailable during work hours and dinner time.

Then stand your ground. Your emotional well-being is just as important as theirs. Sticking to reasonable boundaries is a caring and respectful response.

And seek reciprocity. Relationships work best when both parties are willing to give and take, even though the balance may fluctuate over time. If you find you're constantly getting the short end of the stick, don't be afraid to quit. Some people will only get the message when the letter is marked "return to sender."

Have compassion for yourself and your friends as you work on being there for each other without taking advantage of one another or getting burned out. Good friends care for each. *Close friends* understand each other, *true friends* stay forever, beyond words, beyond distance, beyond time. Do you have close friends or true friends? If neither, then they weren't your friends, so let the relationships end.

Your happiness is worth it!

Break Up Breakthrough

I must admit that I watch a lot of reality television programs and there is a common theme with several characters of the shows—they either have fractured relationships or are mourning the loss of a relationship, which becomes their focus throughout the series.

If this is your reality, believe that you *can* heal. The following steps will help:

1. It's natural to feel sad or angry soon after a relationship ends. But don't stay there. Process your feelings. It's important to get in touch with your emotions. Be gentle with yourself while you're establishing a new routine.

2. Build your self-esteem. Remind yourself of your talents and accomplishments. Their loss is someone else's gain. You can also find comfort and wisdom in your spiritual practices.

3. Spot patterns in your break up history. Determine if your relationships share any commonalities that you would like to change or develop further to improve the chances of building and keeping a relationship that is right for you.

4. Sometimes others can see the situation more clearly than you do and provide you with a

perspective that you hadn't considered regarding your relationships. Accept objective feedback to be open to a healing heart.

5. Don't sit around moping. Spend time with friends. Compassion and support will make the transition time more comfortable.

Break through after a break up and get ready for a new, healthy relationship and improve your chances for success.

You Matter

Appreciating the innate value and worth of every person we encounter is explained through a true story adapted from a 1996 edition of *Guideposts*. A college professor decided to give his class a pop quiz. Most of his students were very conscientious students and breezed through most of the questions—until they read the last, "What is the first name of the woman who cleans the school?"

Surely this is some kind of joke, they thought. Most had seen the cleaning woman several times. She was tall, had dark-hair, and was in her 50s; but few knew her name. Most handed in their papers, leaving the last question blank. Just before class ended, one student asked if the last question would count toward the quiz grade.

"Absolutely," said the professor. "In your careers, you will meet many people. All are significant. They deserve your attention and care, even if all you do is smile and say hello. Everyone, regardless of status or title, matters." Many have never forgotten that lesson.

You may be the cleaning lady, but you have a purpose. You may be the student. You too have a purpose. I experienced this first hand in a discussion with a receptionist at a medical facility. She shared that she was "only" front desk support. Perhaps she felt intimidated by working with others that held titles and degrees in medicine. I shared that she is so much more than a receptionist. She is the first face people see when they enter the business. She sets the atmosphere of how they experience their medical visit. She has power to influence their attitude and perception through her engagement. And she is important.

It doesn't matter who you are, what you do or how difficult life may seem, you matter!

Zip It

"Margaret" mentioned that sometimes success has slipped away because of her "motor mouth." Indeed, sometimes a slip of the tongue can set you back and destroy opportunities for growth. It is important to know when to zip it so you don't get zapped:

1. *Zip it after you ask a question.* Do you know people who ask questions but can't wait for you to finish so they can offer their own viewpoint? Uh huh? When they asked for advice, what they really meant was, "Let's fast-forward to the part where I tell you what I think, instead." Don't be that person. When you close your mouth, your ears get a chance to do their job.

2. *Zip it when you don't know what you're talking about.* Silence is awkward—but don't rush to fill it. You never have to fill a silence, especially when you don't have anything useful to fill it with. Shush don't rush.

3. ***Zip it when your comment is more about you than the other person.*** If someone shares a story or experience with you, be sure that your comments are truly intended to improve the conversation or offer good advice. If there's a chance you're commenting out of jealousy or pride, you're better off zipping it so you don't get zapped.

Knowing when to say what and how is a learned behavior. Keep practicing your listening skills and you will have more success.

Connections

February is the month of love, it's typically called the heart month as we focus on our physical heart with GO RED campaigns sponsored by the American Heart Association or some other organization. We celebrate relationships with words, flowers, chocolates, and other gifts because relationships are vitally important to us. To highlight this point, Bronnie Ware, a nurse in Australia, wrote a book entitled *The Top Five Regrets of the Dying,* based on her experiences listening to people in their last stages of life. A recurring theme revealed through her experiences is the importance of connection with others—our relationships. Bronnie found that a key regret shared by those individuals was letting "things" get in the way of maintaining quality relationships.

Julia Menard published the following three blocks to connections that harm our relationships with others.

The first block is *blaming others for our feelings.* Instead of naming our feelings and expressing our deepest needs stimulating that feeling, we blame the other person for how we feel. Share who you are instead of blaming others—and invite true connection.

Another block to connecting with others is *confusing a solution with a need*. It's helpful to separate our needs from the way we get those needs met. We all have needs—a sense of belonging, love, connection—and these are *nonnegotiable*. But how we get those needs met *is* negotiable. For example, if you want to see the movie and your mate or friend doesn't, it could lead to conflict. However, when each of you realizes the need is for fun and sharing, think of ways to do that staying in instead of going out. It's important to find solutions that meet both person's needs.

A third block to connecting with others is *digging in our heels* and seeing our own solution as the only solution. It happens often in relationships, Instead of the individuals sitting down and discussing their feelings and deeper needs, each person shows up with a solution in mind and imposes that solution to solve the problem. Don't get caught up in a power struggle. Remember, there are always other solutions.

Get rid of the blocks that are in the way of vibrant and connected relationships—at home and in the workplace. Live today so you don't face regret in your relationships tomorrow.

Note

1.   Jakes, T.D. https://www.youtube.com/watch?v=DjnuvrhZ4FU

PART IV

REFRESHMENT

Encourage Yourself

My favorite saying is "To achieve you have to believe," but at times that's easier said than done. If you're stuck in a motivation rut, try these tactics to encourage yourself:

1. *Choose happiness.* Focus on the wonderful things in your life that fill you with gratitude. It's easier to motivate yourself when you're in a positive mood.

1. *Learn to be a finisher.* Incomplete projects can dampen anyone's enthusiasm. Avoid quitting before a task is 100 percent completed. You'll be more interested in taking on new assignments when you expect to be successful.

2. *Lift your motivation by understanding the lessons of your mistakes.* The only people who don't make mistakes are those who never do anything. The more mistakes you make, the more you'll learn and grow.

3. *Keep yourself grounded in the present.* If you're worrying about the future or beating yourself up over the past, it's challenging to get anything accomplished right now. Take things day by day.

4. *Measure your progress.* Big goals or projects can take years to complete. Stay on track with short-term accomplishments to keep you focused and motivated.

Find your fulfillment, learn from your mistakes, and celebrate your success. Encourage yourself from within and begin!

You First

Sometimes we are so busy doing things for others that we neglect our own needs. How many times have you bypassed your own desires for someone else's wants?

It's completely admirable for you to want to financially take care of your family and friends, but it's important to balance that with self-care. Follow these guidelines to balance self-care with other responsibilities:

Begin by *being creative with quiet time.* Instead of foregoing your spa day for babysitting duties or overtime, take your little one with you. Get mom and daughter pedicures or 2 for 1 back massages. That way you're taking care of your loved one and getting well-deserved pampering for yourself! Or schedule your quiet time when everyone else is asleep or otherwise occupied. You'll be tempted to get some chores done, but resist! What's not done today can be done tomorrow.

Get the rest you need. Avoid feeling guilty about taking a break. The world can manage to stay intact for a short time while you rest.

Share your needs with your loved ones. Tell them that you like to feel appreciated. Once they're aware of this, you no longer have to worry about satisfying them on your own. You can comfortably focus on their needs while they focus on yours.

Make yourself a priority. While you're taking care of everyone else at work and at home, don't forget about yourself. It is not selfish to love yourself and put yourself first.

Minimalist Bliss

You may have heard people say, "I need to simplify my life." Or perhaps you've said it yourself. And while simplicity is good, minimalism is better. Simplicity and minimalism are sometimes used interchangeably, yet they are different. Simplicity relates to ease while minimalism literally requires removing things from your life.

If you have items in your way that you rarely use, excessive debt, or feel like your life is too hectic or lacks meaning, minimalist ideas might help you create a life that's more centered and enjoyable.

To introduce minimalism into your life, *take action:*

1. Get rid of clutter. When you pull out scarves, hats, and sweaters for a winter season and find items that you haven't worn for the past three years, don't put them in your drawer telling yourself you will wear them. Let me tell you this—you won't. Put them in the donate pile. Stop fooling yourself. Let it go. Make room for a new sweater and new gifts to come into your life. Do this for all the spaces you live in. Not only will your home or office look cleaner, but you'll be surprised at how much better you feel!

2. Make a list of all the optional activities in your life. Include all the organizations, clubs, team sports, happy hours…Eliminate one. In a couple of weeks, eliminate another. Now fill some of that free time with activities you really love.

3. Consider the things you are doing when you are thinking about doing the things that are most important to you. Then determine what you can do to minimize the time on the tasks. This might include delegation or deletion.

Repeat this process on a regular basis. Just a couple of cycles of minimalizing will dramatically reduce the complexity of your life.

Here are two things to remember if you get stuck in the process:

1. You can do *anything* but not everything—take on only what you can manage.

2. *Someday* is not a day of the week. Set a date. Don't leave it up to chance or when you happen to have time—chances are you won't find the time, so make time to get started.

Life doesn't have a remote. You must get up and change it. Free yourself. It's always in the season to declutter—something new is waiting for you!

Calgon, Take Me Away

In the 1970s a very popular advertisement was introduced which became part of pop culture. The commercial featured a woman standing in front of a screen with annoying images of a noisy traffic jam, an overbearing boss, the screaming baby and barking dog, she puts her hands up in submission and she says, "That does it…Calgon (a water softening solution) take me away!"

We all have "Calgon" moments when we wish we could escape into a warm, relaxing bath. Especially during times of high stress. To escape the mess and reduce the stress try the following:

- **Visualize.** Redirecting your thoughts to calm visions or things that excite you helps to relieve stress. Picture a peaceful scene: a future vacation, your favorite beach. Or you can even visualize yourself accomplishing a future goal.

- **Pucker up.** Kissing relieves stress by helping your brain release endorphins—or as I call them, the warm and fuzzies. Research shows that people who kiss less are more stressed and depressed. Kiss your stress away.

- **Breathe deeply.** It's often said to count to ten when you're angry. The reason, breathing exercises—or even just taking a few deep breaths—can help reduce tension and relieve stress, thanks to an extra boost of oxygen.

- **Laugh.** It's true! Laughter is the best medicine.

- **Spend time with a close friend.** We don't need science to tell us how a smile or conversation with a good friend can turn your frown upside down. Surround yourself with people who will encourage you.

Don't stress. Do your best. Appreciate each step. And forget the rest!

Seven Ways to Enjoy Your Days

Too many people are overworked and exhausted. They are moving but not going anywhere. Finding more time for what we want to do seems impossible. I've got news for you—you don't have to make dramatic steps or carve out chunks of time to enjoy your days in wonderful ways. Try the following seven great ideas to put more enjoyment into every moment:

1. Hug! Try 10 seconds of hugging a child, pet, spouse, or friend. Feel the love and warmth of moment.

2. Right now: Sit up really tall and relax your shoulders. Now take a deep breath. Do it again.

Blow it out and breathe in. Meditate on how you feel in the relaxed moment.

3. Try this—turn your cell phone to silent for a full day. You'll be surprised how relaxing it can be without the constant beeping, vibrating, and ringing of the phone.

4. Teach someone something you are good at. Caring and sharing gives an energy boost to your mind and body.

5. Ever try swapping breakfast for dinner or vice versa. Switch things up and concentrate only on eating with no TV, phone, or computer.

6. Stop whatever you're doing, look around and smell and touch your surroundings. Be more mindful of your surroundings.

7. What are you thankful for right now? As you think, SMILE! One of the easiest ways to boost your health, your mood, your longevity, and even your success is to smile.

Enjoy the moments of your life because living is once, chances are rare, and nothing is certain.

Give Yourself the Green Light

One of the challenges of moving forward is that by human nature we often need approval. Think back to when you were growing up. There was always someone "in charge." Whatever you wanted to do, you had to ask permission first.

But now that we're all grown up, we don't have anyone to really check in with. (Sure there may be a spouse and significant others, and a boss, but that's about courtesy and respect.) When it comes to stepping out of the box and doing what needs to be done to pursue your desires, there's only one person who can give you the "green light" to go ahead and that is *you*.

So what is holding you back from giving yourself permission? There are three common reasons people—perhaps you—put the brakes on fulfilling their dreams.

- **Validation.** It is comforting to have someone agree with our plans and goals. But remember this is *your* dream. It was given to *you*. It has to start with you. A successful journey requires courage and belief in yourself.

- **Need to know it's the right thing.** It may not be the right thing, but allow yourself to try. In order to discover new lands, you *must be willing to lose sight of the shore*. Give yourself permission to go beyond traditional limits.

- **Don't have time.** There's not one person on this earth who has achieved his or her goals without putting in the time. The amount of time you dedicate to your dream is dependent solely on you. It simply comes down to how badly you want it. You cannot get to where you want to be until you commit to your goals. Your goals are like ammunition. They will shoot down obstacles that don't line up with your vision, and you'll be amazed at what you accomplished when it's all said and done.

Don't be discouraged about what others might say; at first they'll ask why you're doing it, but later they'll ask how you did it. Give yourself the green light and achieve the success you desire!

Happiness Advantage

Most people believe that success will bring happiness; but Shawn Achor, a psychology researcher and author of *The Happiness Advantage,* says that while we may think success will bring us happiness, the lab-validated truth is that *happiness brings us more success.* Shawn says to reverse the happiness and success formula. We think if we work harder and achieve some goal, then we'll be happier. But the research is clear that every time you have a success, your brain changes what success means.

So if happiness is on the opposite side of success, you'll never get there. But if you increase your levels of happiness in the midst of a challenge—it has been proven that you will find that all of your success rates rise dramatically. Those who practice the happiness advantage find better and secure jobs, are better keeping jobs, experience superior productivity and business opportunities, and have less burn out.

It's possible because it turns out that the brain works significantly better when you're feeling positive—so developing a sunny outlook allows you to be smarter and more creative.

To increase your happiness quotient, Harvard researchers have found that something as simple as writing down three things you're grateful for every day for twenty-one days in a row significantly increases your level of optimism and it holds for the next six months. The research proves we actually can change.

Start writing, giving, sharing, and keep growing. Increase your happiness and you will increase your success!

Uniquely You

One of the major sources of stress and barriers to success is that individuals have an unhealthy habit of comparing themselves to others. We are all different, but it's human nature to compare. And while learning from others is an important part of decision making, if comparison is used to reinforce an unrealistic or negative self-image, it can be an harmful habit.

To avoid the pitfalls of comparison, take this advice:

1. Get clear about you. A healthy sense of self allows you to appreciate other people's successes and become better, not bitter. List words that describe you: smart, strong, kind, mother, father, friend, visionary. Value yourself and you won't want to be like someone else.

2. Seek meaning, not approval. Don't spend life chasing recognition. Work to advance your dreams, then your place in the pecking order ceases to matter.

3. Know your strengths. Don't measure what you do by what others have done. You don't know their story. You have your own unique gifts and talents.

4. Emulate what works. I always say it's all right to be a copycat, just be sure you're copying the right cat. When someone does something well, assess what was done and figure out how to

incorporate those traits into your life. No need
to reinvent the wheel all of the time.

It's easy to believe that the grass might be greener on the
other side when comparing yourself to others, but you don't
know the cost of their water bill. We were all made as unique
beings with a purpose placed specifically in each of us.

True satisfaction comes from doing your best, not comparing yourself to others. Always remember that you are uniquely
and wonderfully made…flaws and all.

Kill Kinda

Do you kinda want a new relationship? Do you kinda want
a change in your career? Do you kinda want to start something
new but keep getting distracted?

Kinda is ruining dreams, halting momentum, kicking
doors shut and barricading you in a comfort cocoon. The thing
about kinda is that it doesn't care. Kinda loves indecision.
Because all you kinda do is talk about what you want but kinda
doesn't allow you to get there.

Until you replace kinda with a kickstart you'll never
leave your mark. Change the meaning to reflect what you
are dreaming.

To kill kinda –

- **K**eep your goals alive
- **I**gnite your fire to pursue what you're passion-
ate about
- **N**ever stay still – not for a moment
- **D**edicate yourself to a new experience everyday

- **A**llow yourself to get comfortable with discomfort

At times when you kind of feel lost or feel bored or kind of feel like you can't keep going, remember YOU CAN never expect to succeed if you only put in the work on the days you feel like it. There will be obstacles, there will be mistakes and there will be doubts. But with consistency and hard work, there are no limits.

Kill Kinda and keep going!

Don't Give Up

Cathy Hughes, a single mother and now owner of the multibillion dollar media company, Radio One lost everything before her success. For eighteen months, she was homeless and slept in a sleeping bag in the radio station. Cathy said she approached thirty-two men for a business loan with no success. After giving her thirty-third presentation, a woman who was on her first week at the job gave her the loan. What would have happened if she gave up after the thirty-second rejection?

In his first screen test, it is reported that the casting director of MGM told Fred Astaire, "You can't act. Can't sing, slightly bald. Can dance a little." As everyone knows, Fred Astaire became an incredibly successful actor, singer, and dancer. But what if he quit after hearing that disheartening critique?

Whatever you're going through, creating, or trying to achieve, don't give up. You could be one step away from your breakthrough, one yes away from that loan approval, one interview away from that new job, one encounter away from meeting your soulmate.

While waiting:

1.   Be of good cheer. Operate in a spirit of expectation. It is true your actions follow your thoughts. If you expect things will work out in your favor, your activities are poised in that direction.

2.   Learn as much as you can. Continue to improve by seeking information and talent and connect with others for skill-building and encouragement.

Don't be afraid of failing. Most people would be surprised to learn that Michael Jordan was actually cut from his high school basketball team. He is quoted as saying, "I have missed more than 9,000 shots in my career. I have lost almost 300 games. On 26 occasions I have been entrusted to take the game-winning shot, and I missed. I have failed over and over and over again in my life. And that is why I succeed."

Have FAITH not fear and you will get there! Believe!

The Present

As a little girl, I remember visiting my grandmother who delighted in the new furniture she bought that was covered completely in plastic. On hot summer days I got stuck on it and had to peel free from the plastic. And through time, when the plastic was tearing at the seams, Grandmom patched it with tape. Many years later, when my grandmother passed away, my aunts took the plastic off and the fabric of the furniture was still like new. And I realized then that my grandmother never really enjoyed the beauty or comfort of the furniture. I always wondered, *Why buy it if you're not going to benefit from it?*

Too often we are saving something for a special occasion, a rainy day, or just the exact right time. But what if that special occasion doesn't happen, or it doesn't rain, or you don't find the right time? The fact is, every day of life is a special occasion. Don't put off for tomorrow what you can enjoy today. Life doesn't have to be perfect to be wonderful. Just imagine if you began every day with the thought, *Today is going to be the best day of my life!* What would you do differently? What would you celebrate? The answers are what you should be doing.

I encourage you to never get so busy trying to make a living that you forget to live life. Don't wish away your days waiting for better ones. Remember, yesterday is history, tomorrow is a mystery, but today is a gift of God, which is why we call it the present.

Back to Basics

I enjoyed junior high school. One of my favorite classes was creative writing. As students we were encouraged to write and express our emotions and the things we were imagining or experiencing. I believe this is one reason that led me into a life of journaling. Whether you've had a creative writing course or not, you can use this art to process your emotions and reduce stress.

Visual journaling enables you to articulate your feelings. When you're struggling to put your emotions into words, it may be easier to sketch them out. To realize your personal goals and increase your willpower, add visual journaling as part of your strategy for moving ahead in life.

1. *Create your journal.* To create your journal, doodle a little. Free-form doodling may uncover

your subconscious concerns about your career, health, or family.

2. *Assemble a collage.* Browse through magazines for pictures and create your own design.

Each time you update your journal, you remind yourself about the positive changes you are trying to achieve. It's a simple way to create triggers that reinforce new habits that help *manage stress without any extra calories or financial expense.*

Take it back to basics with visual journaling to lift your spirits, clarify your thinking, and as motivation to increase opportunities for your success. Creative expression is good for your health and well-being.

Move It to Improve It

It's been proven that sitting too much is bad for your health. In a recent study, researchers found some startling results: not only are people with sitting jobs 54 percent more likely to die of a heart attack, but your daily hour of gym time isn't enough to compensate for the eight (or more like eleven) hours you spend at your desk.

And while standing desks, walking meetings, and treadmill desks have popped up as common remedies to combat the inactive office lifestyle, the real solution might be simpler than you think. You can make a few small changes—even if you're chained to your desk all day—to improve your posture and (seriously) boost your health. Accomplish it by:

- Practice active sitting. This goes against most of what I learned as a little girl, but try not to cross your legs, which can restrict circulation.

- Don't sit in a chair that is rigid for an extended period of time. Being able to rock back and forth in your chair is helpful to your body and mind. Recent studies show rocking improves concentration.

- Interrupt your sitting at least once every thirty minutes. Do some shoulder shrugs (lift your shoulders up to your neck and relax them down). Also, get up and do calf-raising exercises (lift up on your tippy toes and relax down) both of these simple exercises will loosen your joints, relieve tension, and stretch your muscles.

It's important to take advantage of every chance you have to move your body. Promote your well-being and boost your energy by simply paying more attention to your body during the workday. Get up and move around. It's a simple way to have more success today!

Enrich, Embrace, and Be You

Although many of my clients have increased their level of self-awareness, a barrier that some of them faced was accepting themselves. Although your uniqueness is a blessing, you may find discomfort in the trying to fit in. Maybe you feel discomfort about being different from everyone else. Or perhaps you find yourself similar to others to the point that you believe you're boring.

Either way, it's time to recognize that your special variety of character traits combine to create a one and only, a very unique you.

To discover the amazing individual you are:

1. Take note of your habits. Do you floss your teeth every night and consistently wash the dishes as soon as you dirty them? Is your bedtime always the same?

2. Understand what's important to you by noticing your routine behaviors. In a sense, your habits are your "trademark."

3. A wonderful technique for embracing your individuality is to think deeply about the kind of person you are. If you had to describe yourself to another human being, what words would you use? Maybe you're always in a hurry or like to keep a very clean desk, car, or house. Perhaps you have a lot of friends and are quite gregarious.

4. Write down your description of yourself and be as thoughtful and thorough about your personality characteristics as you can. You're worth the time this strategy will take.

To accept and embrace who you are:

- Identify your biggest struggles. What challenges you? If you're ever stumped about how to handle a situation, describe those situations on paper. Getting a handle on what taxes you most increases your self-awareness.

- Embrace your individuality by accepting who you are. Learning to love yourself and taking yourself as you are is a great aid to loving and

encouraging others. Sure you have flaws, everyone does!

- Love and accept yourself for who you are. Be
positive, be awesome, grateful and become better.

Say Goodbye to Work Guilt

Most parents work to provide comfortably for their fami-
lies but part of that involves some sacrifice that can manifest
as guilt. Maybe you want to spend more time with your kids
or maybe you're concerned about how it looks when you put in
fewer hours than the person in the next cubicle.

Whatever is causing your guilt trip, there is a cure. Try the
following tips for eliminating useless regrets and enjoying more
job satisfaction.

1. Focus on quality time. You can be a super par-
    ent even if you're too booked up to attend every
    soccer practice or bake 500 cupcakes. Make the
    hours you spend together count by sharing your
    love and wisdom with your children.

2. Serve as a role model. Women whose moth-
    ers worked outside the home are more likely to
    be employed and earn higher wages than those
    whose mothers stayed home fulltime, according
    to a Harvard Business School study of twenty-
    four countries. Studies also show that working
    mothers tend to be happier, and that's a positive
    influence on children.

3. Ask for support. Balancing work and fami-
    ly responsibilities is a team effort. Divide up

household chores. Take turns with other parents for babysitting or driving kids to the movies.

4.   Negotiate less overtime. Win your boss over by talking about how to reduce overtime costs. Investments in technology and training may help your company save money while shortening your work week.

5.   Resist comparisons. Are you happy working part time or following an unconventional career path? Create your own definition of success instead of worrying about how you stack up against the rest of your graduating class.

6.   Develop outside interests. It's easier to keep work in perspective when you're well-rounded. Interact with others from a wide variety of backgrounds. Devote your leisure time to learning and helping others.

Dump your guilt so you can savor your time at home without feeling like you're neglecting your work, and vice versa. Clarifying your priorities and managing your time effectively will help you be guilt-free around the clock.

Banish Bad Days

You have good days and bad. But wouldn't it be great if you could eliminate most of the bad days from your life? You have the ability to *make good days the norm*. It all depends on what you label a day as "good." If you need help in banishing bad days, try these tips:

Simply REFUSE to have a bad day. You might be running late, your car decides to break down, or someone might speak rudely to you. Avoid the temptation to let these mishaps ruin your day. Take some deep breaths, quickly collect your thoughts, laugh at the devil, and keep it moving. In spite of whatever is going wrong, *you* decide your day. Release your expectations and try to find the good in each situation.

Try doing less. Reduce your schedule to the most important tasks. Having too much to do creates many challenges that get in the way of having a good day. Complete urgent tasks and reschedule the rest.

And finally, *be grateful.* When life is wearing you down, remember all the great things in your life. Give yourself a few minutes to list all the positive people and circumstances in your life. Are you healthy? Do you have friends and family? Your life is probably much better than you think!

Having a good day is relative. Only you can assign a quality label to your day. *Make the conscious decision to have a great every day* and banish the bad days away.

Refillable

People who wonder whether the glass is half empty or half full miss the point. The glass is refillable. Even in your toughest times be mindful that opportunity can be just one meeting, one personal connection, one email, or phone call away. When you transform your thinking to what could be versus what was or is, you attract success not mess.

Much of how we feel about ourselves, others, and even life is the consequence of our thoughts.

In his letter to the Philippians, Saint Paul, wrote, "Think on these things. Whatever is true. Whatever is right. Whatever is lovely."

To change your thinking involves awareness. Know first what it is you are thinking. Be the observer of your thoughts. I cannot stress more strongly that you are not your thoughts. You are instead, the observer of your thoughts. Train yourself to observe the thoughts that randomly come into your mind. This creates a little separation between you, the real you, and the thoughts you are thinking.

When life throws you a curve ball do you immediately think, "I'll never get ahead". Condition your brain to see the good in the situation. Instead think, "I've experienced a setback but I can rebound". This takes practice. Think on purpose.

When you hear distressful news immediately take deep breaths...Try not to respond immediately. Give yourself a few seconds or even minutes to process the news. And repeat to yourself, "this is only a temporary situation. Trouble doesn't last always. I can handle this."

Then think of the best ways to overcome the situation. Forward thinking removes mental barriers and allows you to absorb stress in a less negatively impactful way.

A conscious shift in how and what you think can change your life forever—for the better!

Fight Fatigue

As an entrepreneur and busy professional, fatigue was more common in my vocabulary than I liked. Then I learned something wonderful! If you want fight fatigue, try yoga. Yes, yoga!

Now I'm not an "exercise person," if there is such a thing; but a study by the University of Ohio adds to the evidence that yoga improves sleep.

If you want to have more energy, check out these four ways yoga fights fatigue:

- Yoga frees your mind and body from common obstacles to sleep. As unpleasant thoughts and body aches diminish, you feel more rested.

- Yoga also has a spiritual dimension. Mindfulness and breathing practices promote peace of mind and greater resilience.

- Yoga helps to strengthen your cardiovascular system by stimulating the flow of blood and oxygen through all the cells of your body. Experienced yoga practitioners often develop low resting heart rates, which is a good measure of overall fitness and strongly associated with a longer life span.

- Yoga helps to make you more flexible. That may be especially important if you sit all day for work. Increased flexibility unblocks your energy and gives you more power.

Always look for improvements and solutions. Yoga worked for me. I'm a fighter and fatigue is no longer winning this battle.

Everyday Simplicity

Do you feel like life is too hectic to enjoy? *By removing the things from your life that don't matter and adding things that do, life can be much simpler and more enjoyable.* There are a few daily habits that can make a big difference in creating more simplicity in your life. To remove much of the clutter and distractions from your daily life:

1. Put things away when you're finished with them. Everything that you have to pick up and put away is something that someone failed to put back in the proper place. Enforce this rule with all members of your family and coworkers at your workplace.

2. Sit down and pay your bills each week. Knowing you have bills due weighs on your mind, whether you realize it or not. Take care of them regularly.

3. My husband constantly reminds me to keep the gas tank at least half-full. If your tank is always at least half-full, you can get gas at your leisure. How convenient!

4. Spend fifteen minutes picking up the house each night and cleaning your desk before you leave work for the day. At home, make it a ritual for the entire family. Set a timer and have a race to see who can get the most done.

5. Create a basic filing system. At home, at the very least, assign a file drawer in a desk to organize your important papers, bills, and anything else that needs to be saved. At work, ensure that your filing system is organized for easy access and retrieval of materials.

6. And last, get ready for work or school the night before. Rather than rushing around in the morning making lunches and searching for papers or clean clothes, your preparation can lead to elation. Your mornings will be much more peaceful.

You'll notice that simplifying your life is mostly about doing a few simple things each day. *It only takes a few new habits to enhance your life and create a greater sense of well-being.* Simplicity doesn't require a complicated system. Simplicity should just be simple.

Time to Play

Consider the following lines from a poem found in Viola Walden's book, *Under Construction: Pardon the Mess.*

My precious boy with the golden hair
Came up one day beside my chair
And fell upon his bended knee
And said, "Oh, Mommy, play with me!"
I said, "Not now, go on and play;
I've got so much to do today."
But the chores lasted all through the day
And I never did find time to play.
When supper was over and dishes done,
I was much too tired for my little son.
I tucked him in and kissed his cheek
And watched my angel fall asleep.
As I tossed and turned upon my bed,
Those words kept ringing in my head,

"Not now, son, go on and play,
I've got so much to do today."
I fell asleep and in a minute's span,
My little boy is a full-grown man.
No toys are there to clutter the floor;
No dirty fingerprints on the door;
No snacks to fix; no tears to dry;
The rooms just echo my lonely sigh.
And now I've got the time to play;
But my precious boy is gone away.

This poem is an analogy of our journey through life. What things have you put off for another day? You've thought about starting a catering business with your grandmother's recipes but had no time to plan. You dreamed about starting a career in real estate, but had no time to prepare for the exam. You set goals to finish your degree, but had no time study.

The reality is, there will never be the right time or enough time. But it's better to live with failures because you tried than to live a life of regret. I encourage you to live a life by design, rather than default. Decide today that you will find the time to play.

Body Language

Does the following sound familiar? You've had your eye on a promotion. The choice is between you and your colleague. You put in crazy hours and take on extra projects. But when the promotion is announced, it goes to your colleague instead. What went wrong? The reason you didn't get the job may not be related to your work but instead due to your body language.

Your body language can have a big impact on the way you are perceived by others because it is a way we express ourselves. Try these techniques to improve your success:

1. Don't cross your arms in front. Many people take that position out of habit, but it is actually a defensive position. To others this may come off as cynical, distrustful, and even that you are angry. Instead, stand with your arms by your side, slightly out from your body, which shows openness and confidence.

2. Don't seem disinterested. Show engagement in conversations by mimicking and mirroring others' gestures. If they place their hands on the table do the same. If they lean slightly back in their chairs, do the same. This expresses harmony and interest.

3. Be aware of nervous gestures. Jiggling legs, hair twirling, face touching, etc. signal insecurity. Control your movements by placing your hands on the table or in your lap if sitting, on your hips, or holding a notebook.

4. Look people in the eye. Poor eye contract can be misunderstood as lacking confidence. Try holding a person's gaze for 50-60 percent of the time you're interacting with them. If you can master this, chances are others will perceive you as confident and sure of yourself.

5. Shake well. Engage with a good, confident handshake that is neither too firm nor too light.

The sense of touch is incredibly important for conveying rapport.

It's important to know what you don't know in order to improve. Increase opportunities for your success in any setting by adapting these body language techniques.

Let the Games Begin

Some believe that fate determines their lives. Others abide by the expression, "Life is what you make it." Although it's fine to believe in fate, if you want something different, exhilarating, or exciting in life, it might not work out so well to sit around waiting for fate to produce it. Instead, why not see your life as something you have a hand in crafting?

To create more adventure in your life, stop taking the path of least resistance or better known as the "safe" route. Live life as if you won't get a second chance. Refrain from shying away from challenges that might beset you if you truly feel that great rewards will come in the future. Frankly, it could all be over tomorrow. What would you regret not doing?

Instead of the usual path, carve out a new highway leading to your success. Don't be afraid of the hairpin curves or steep, climbing stretches. You might be surprised what's on the other end of your journey.

Generate a list of least likely options. For example, if you have options of either taking a nine-month certification course to become a medical assistant or two years of night school to become an x-ray technician, look closely at your least likely option so you can take into account the journey, adventure, and long-term payoff of each choice.

Choose the journey that deep down you think you can't do—but really want to do. Maybe you're worried about getting the school loan for the two-year educational program and you know the time constraints will be tough, but in the back of your mind you still want to go for it. It's time to opt for what is really calling you, deep inside. It might be the greatest ride of your life! And who knows who you might encounter along the way.

Get in the game of life. Don't just be a spectator. Go beyond your comfort zone. Be true to you and pursue!

Happiness Is Free

Most people think they would be happy if they had more "stuff" or more money. A better car or a better house sounds pretty good to most people. Having more money and stuff may make things easier, but they don't necessarily provide happiness.

There are four things that *do* bring happiness, and the best part—they're free!

It doesn't cost anything to love. Everyone needs someone to love. If you don't think you have someone to love, go find someone. The world is full of people who feel unloved, so it shouldn't take you too long to find a volunteer. We all need someone to cherish and care for. Caring for others instantly provides more happiness. And if you're not comfortable with people, adopt a pet. Furry companions can brighten your day in amazing ways.

It's free to have something to look forward to. Switch out of the same, boring daily routines. What is something you'd really like to do or see? Maybe it is something as simple as an exercise class or book club. Or perhaps, if you love going the movies on Friday nights, it can make your mid-week Wednesdays a little easier when you know that movie night is looming in your future.

Perhaps your biggest challenge is dealing with downtime. When you're bored, lonely, anxious, or sad and don't have anything to do, it's easy to resort to watching TV, surfing the internet, eating when you aren't hungry, shopping for stuff you don't really want or need. Here's a secret: using downtime in more joyful ways doesn't have to cost a thing! Pause before you go on autopilot, then choose to read something worthwhile, go for a jog or brisk walk, meet up with a friend and do something fun, make a new friend, or work on a hobby.

But most of all, learn to be happy—not because everything is good, but because you can see the good in everything.

The One-Day Vacay

Towards the end of my corporate career, I sought ways to refresh and rejuvenate my mind and spirit by taking breaks. Breaks are essential for improving health, productivity, and happiness. I was relentless to ensure to use break time to its full advantage. If you only have one day to totally unwind, relax, and unplug, here's some advice for making the most of just a little time off.

- First, give yourself permission to invest in "you time," even if it means doing absolutely nothing. It is crucial to understand that personal time is a priority, not an option.

- Watch out for feelings of guilt that sneak their way into your brain. Once you've taken the day off, make enjoying that time your goal.

- Choose a day when fewer people are out and about trying to get their own to-do lists done. Less distractions can equate to more relaxation.

- Spend time with friends and family you don't normally get to see during the workday to feel extra rejuvenated.

- Completely unwind by doing anything and everything unproductive: watch a movie, visit a bookstore, play solitaire, or take a long nap. Life doesn't always have to be so serious.

- Schedule your extra day off on a Friday or Monday and turn your one day into a mini-weekend getaway! Visit a nearby park or museum or library.

Don't wait for a sick day to rest. Take a one-day vacay to refocus, recharge, and regain strength for everyday living.

Love Strong—Live Long

Most people want to live to be 100. It seems to be the magic number for a long, prosperous life. But 100 years on the planet is very different from loving life each of those 100 years. Here are a few things you can do to love strong and live long (adapted from lifehack.org).

1. Love unconditionally. As you get older, many of the things that you find most appealing today

won't even be a huge part of your future. Your job will consume less of your life and your looks will fade, but your relationships with family and friends will endure. Take time with those you love. Maintain the bond and hold on to those close to you. Don't allow petty problems to drive a wedge into relationships. A loving, caring support system shines through when other things fade.

2. Embrace the changes that age brings. I awoke last week to four new grey hairs. I embraced them as a sign of my wisdom and maturity. That was a more fulfilling feeling than fussing over them. My father realized that he's not as good as he used to be at remembering things. He found comfort in the fact that he can use his mobile phone to record messages as reminders. Don't let grey hairs or wrinkles or other changes rule you; rather, make the most of your experiences.

3. Play chess, Monopoly, or checkers. That's right… play games. Keep your mind sharp and maintain a competitive edge. Learning to love these types of strategy games when you're young will give you something to excel at as you age. Alertness will make your days full, no matter what stage in life.

4. Travel; learn to love being away from home. Learn to love adventure. Many things will change in your lifetime. Be open to all the experiences that 100 years can bring. Travel the

world. Or better yet, explore your surroundings. Find things outside of your home that you love and embrace them.

You'll find that 100 years will fly by when you live each one like it's your last. Love strong and live long. Enjoy the journey of life!

Savor the Moments

Finding pleasure in life plays a very important role in our happiness. Our happiness is about "feeling good" and having positive and pleasurable experiences. The more pleasure, the better. Some believe that seeking pleasure can't truly bring happiness, because we are always chasing after our next desire, like a drug addict looking for the next fix.

According to science, both of these views have some validity. Studies on the nature of pleasure are now revealing exactly how we can make the most of pleasure in our lives and its relationship to our overall happiness. Here are the main findings published by Steven Handel:[1]

- **Moderate your pleasurable experiences.** These experiences are more valuable when we are able to abstain from them for short periods of time. This is because our pleasure often follows a law of diminishing returns: the first piece of cake you eat tastes better than the second one; and as you eat more, it becomes less and less pleasurable to you. Being able to moderate our pleasurable experiences allows us to appreciate them more when they happen.

- **Treat moments as if they are your last.** A study found that participants were more likely to rate a piece of chocolate as more pleasurable when told it was their "last one" rather than their "next one." When we think something is going to be our last experience, we try to make the most out of it, thus we're more motivated to savor it. Imagine if we treated all of our pleasure experiences as if they could be our last? This attitude could help us make the most of every experience.

- **Focus on positive sensations.** All pleasure boils down to a physical experience through our senses, like sight, sound, taste, smell, or touch. Meditation is a great exercise to become more attuned to our body and senses. Studies prove that disciplined meditation can have a real effect on heightening our senses and the way we process our experiences.

Whether you believe the science or not, the purpose is to savor the moments. If you're living in the fast lane, you still have to slow down and pull over at times to gas up. Try using the pleasure pump and experience happiness and fulfillment in life.

The Rest Is Yet to Come!

There is one element of my life that is very important to my sanity. When it is lacking, I'm moody and irritable. I'm off-balance. Literally, I can't even think straight. I'm talking about sleep. I have learned that in order for me to be focused, productive, and positive, I need to get enough rest.

Studies prove that rest is vital to our mental, physical, and spiritual health. When you sleep, your brain recharges so that you wake up alert and clear-headed. Your self-control, attention, and memory are all reduced when you don't get enough—or the right kind—of sleep.

Our brains are very fickle when it comes to sleep. To wake up feeling rested, your brain needs to move through an elaborate series of cycles. You can help this process along and improve the quality of your sleep by eating and living better—this means reducing stress, exercising, limiting caffeine intake, and all that other good stuff we hear that we should be doing.

You might need to make changes to your usual routine so you can rest more to be your best more often! Instead of talking with friends for an hour at the lunch table, find a place of rest for a few minutes before resuming work. A 20-minute nap is more rejuvenating than 200 mg of caffeine or a bout of exercise. Another study found that a 40-minute nap improves alertness 100 percent.

Rest will improve your performance, leading to greater success in your life! The best is yet to come when rest is part of the recipe.

Note

1. Steven Handel, "How to Savor the Moment: Scientific Ways to Increase Pleasure in Your Life," February 9, 2013; http://www.theemotionmachine.com/how-to-savor-the-moment-scientific-ways-to-increase-pleasure-in-your-life/; accessed March 21, 2017.

PART V

CONFIDENCE

Confidence Boosters

These are a few events that can make us incredibly nervous like a job interview, big client meeting, critical presentation, pitching an idea to your boss, or meeting your partner's family for the first time. This can be emotionally paralyzing. Oftentimes what's needed to move forward is a quick dose of confidence to overcome the temporary anxiety. The following are three ways to help you boost your confidence:

1. **Know what you know.** Create a pattern of behaviors that helps you prepare and emotionally center yourself. Practice interview questions just before the meeting, and review the pitch you are going to make to your boss a few minutes beforehand. This way your ideas are fresh and at the forefront of your thoughts. When you know what you know, you're more comfortable and your confidence will increase.

2. **Prepare for "What if."** *What if they ask me a question I can't answer? What if they don't like my ideas?* The "What ifs" can be a big worry. Think about a few of the worst things that can happen and create a plan to deal with them. Fear of the unknown is a confidence killer that can quickly spiral out of control. Simply going through the exercise of planning for different scenarios will make you better prepared to think on your feet and adapt if the unexpected does occur.

3. **Burn off some chemical stress.** When you feel anxious or stressed, your adrenal glands secrete cortisol. Loosen up with controlled breathing or exercises. Take deep breaths or take a walk. Why not try some stretching exercises just before the meeting. It can give you the boost of confidence you need to succeed.

Melanie Koulouris reminds us to be humble in confidence yet courageous in character. This is only a bump in the road and you're belted in for the long haul. You can do it!

To Believe or Not to Believe

Over the years through various interactions. I have learned that the reason some people don't succeed in achieving their goals isn't because of lack of resources, finances, or abilities. But rather the *inaccurate beliefs they have about success.* If your ideas about success are faulty, that can lead to inappropriate action or even worst, no action at all.

Misperceptions regarding success include the beliefs that:

- **You must be smart to succeed.** Actually, the opposite may be true. Consistency and determination are far more important than intelligence when it comes to success. In fact, researcher carried out by the Carnegie Institute of Technology shows that 85% of your financial success is determined by your personality, and ability to communicate, lead, and negotiate.

- **Another misperception is that you need an original idea.** That's not so true. Many people are successful as EBay retailers selling old items from their garages or flea markets. And remember the tae bo craze? Billy Blanks didn't invent exercising, just another way to get fit and have fun doing it.

- **You need a lot of money.** Not always! Christopher Johnson invented the ramen noodle cooker with a $500 investment. In three years, he made millions selling a microwave bowl.

- **It takes time.** This is probably the most common misperception. Here's the reality:

we all have the same twenty-four hours each day. The question is, "Are you spending your twenty-four hours as effectively as possible?" It boils down to how bad you want it and what you are willing to do to make it happen.

Believe what you want…where there's a will, there's a way. You choose!

Bravery

Cowardly lions aren't the only ones who wonder what their lives would be like if they had more courage. *Imagine standing up for your convictions and taking risks to go after the things that are important to you.*

There are two major schools of thought about courage. You might act boldly because you are fearless. On the other hand, you might feel anxious, but forge ahead anyway because you decide that the rewards are worth it.

Either way, *courage is a skill that you can cultivate.* Use these steps to build your faith to conquer your doubts and face the things that scare you.

Step 1: Value yourself. Bravery comes down to making yourself vulnerable because the rewards justify taking the risk. Ask yourself how far you'll go to live out your dreams.

Step 2: Believe in your abilities. Reflect on your past accomplishments and understand your potential.

Step 3: Select inspiring role models to build your faith. It's good to have heroes. Find a mentor who has the qualities you want to possess. It may be your college professor, a work colleague, or a character in your favorite novel or on a TV show. Then model their behavior.

Step 4: Take action. You don't know what your capabilities are until you try. Yet it is important to be sensible. Being courageous is different from being reckless. Plan ahead so you'll be ready to deal with the outcomes of your decisions.

There's a saying that a ship is safe in the harbor, but that's not what ships are for. What do you stand for? Move forward in spite of your fears. You are stronger, smarter, and braver than you think.

Rejection or Redirection?

Getting rejected, whether for a career position or in a relationship, can be one of the most challenging events you'll ever experience. So it may be hard to believe that there is a rainbow at the end of the storm when it comes to rejection, but it's true! There are some positive aspects about being rejected if you look for the plus instead of disgust. Here's the deal, chances are:

1. You get a "do over." A rejection likely signals an end of something. Perhaps it's the end of going through a tedious process of a job search or the end of a relationship. Whatever the case, when a rejection occurs, something new is about to begin. Maybe you will settle back into your current job with renewed efforts.

2. Another revelation is that you have time to reflect on the rejection. Figure out what role you may have played in the situation. Consider your behavior, your actions, and how you might have

affected others throughout whatever transpired before and during the rejection—this can be quite revealing.

3. Take the opportunity to learn anything you can change about yourself after a rejection—it's good to refocus on you for a while.

4. Don't stay stuck in rejection. Take the bull by the horns and make some plans for your future. What goals do you have? What do you need to be doing right now to get closer to achieve them? Use the clarity you have after the rejection to motivate you.

5. Strive to get to the point where you can say, "It was worth it!" Every life experience gives us something—because everything happens on purpose for a purpose. You will be able to move forward more confidently with that mindset!

Soon you will proclaim, "Every time I thought I was being rejected, I was actually being redirected to something better!"

When Things Go Wrong

With concerns about climate change and seemingly rapid or unnatural fluctuations in the weather, there are storms throughout regions broadcast daily on the news. During these times, many people lost electricity, forcing them to seek shelter with relatives or hotels. Multiple car accidents were reported. And businesses lost significant revenues due to closures. Whether within our control or not, things *will* go wrong. When things go wrong in your life and you need support to stay on track, remember:

Everything in life is temporary. Every time it rains, it eventually stops raining. Every time you get hurt, you heal. So if things are good right now, enjoy it. It won't last forever. If things are bad, don't worry, because it won't last forever either. Just because life isn't easy doesn't mean you have to be miserable. Every moment gives you a new beginning and a new ending. You get a second chance, every second. Take it and make the best of it.

Other people's negativity is not your problem. Be positive when negativity surrounds you or when others try to bring you down. It's an easy way to maintain your enthusiasm and focus. Don't let someone else's bitterness change the person you are. Rarely do people do things because of you. They do things because of them.

What's meant to be will eventually, BE. There are blessings hidden in every struggle you face, but you have to be willing to open your heart and mind to see them. You can't force things to happen. You'll only drive yourself crazy trying. At some point you have to let go and let what's meant to be, BE.

In all, trust your intuition, take chances, cherish the memories, and learn through experience. Life is a long-term journey. Laugh at the confusion, live in the moments, and enjoy your life as it unfolds. You might not end up exactly where you intended to go, but you will eventually arrive precisely where you need to be.

When things go wrong, don't go with them. Do what makes you happy and be with whomever makes you smile, often.

Love It or List It

One of my favorite TV shows broadcasts on the Home and Garden channel is called *Love It or List It.* The show is centered on homeowners who are trying to figure out if they will love their own home after repairs or if they will list their home and purchase a new one that is more accommodating to their lifestyle. It's usually a difficult choice for the homeowners. Usually during the renovation process of their current dwelling the homeowners encounter unforeseen structural problems or some issue that frustrates the process. And finding a new house based on their budget, location and availability presents a different set of challenges.

This show is a metaphor for life. We are constantly making decisions. Choosing to stay where you are or deciding to find a new home, even though it may be outside your comfort neighborhood is similar to considerations when contemplating a career move.

There are three simple rules to consider when making decisions:

1. If you don't go after what you want, you'll never have it. Have confidence in yourself and your abilities to pursue the things you desire. There will be obstacles and challenges. You've got what it takes but sometimes it may take all you've got. Don't quit!

2. If you don't ask, the answer is always no. You have a 50/50 chance of getting a yes. Yes to the promotion. Yes to the loan! Yes to the new job! Go get your yes!

3. If you don't step forward, you'll always be in the same place. Every journey starts with a single step. Always believe something wonderful is about to happen and *keep going!*

Filler Up

In general, do you tend to see the glass half full or half empty when faced with challenges or stagnation? If your response is half full, then you're an optimist. Studies show that optimists live longer, achieve more, and enjoy greater happiness and health. But even if you tend to see the glass as half empty, you can tap into these advantages.

Psychologists believe that about 50 percent of your optimist quotient is determined at birth. That leaves the remaining 50 percent that you can work on.

To become more optimistic:

1. Create a distraction. That's right! When you find yourself dwelling on the size of your thighs or how slowly traffic is moving, switch your attention to something more entertaining. Sing your favorite song or remember fun moments with others.

2. Count your blessings—gratitude reinforces optimism. Keep a gratitude list and post it somewhere you can see it all day.

3. Challenge your assumptions. Transform your negative self-talk by arguing the opposing side when you start to criticize yourself. Remember, we're inclined to remember the worst of things

more than the best of times. It's no coincidence that you can more easily recall what went wrong rather than the things that went right.

Seeing the glass half full is possible when you plan ahead. Feeling in control boosts optimism. Clarify your goals and strategies to make it easier to anticipate obstacles and persevere. As your successes add up, the process will become more automatic.

Train yourself to become more hopeful so you can head in the right direction with more energy, clarity, and focus. Believe you can and you will.

Losers Win

If you want to achieve greater success, know that there will be times of failure; that is part of life. You can choose to allow failure to affect your state of mind or you can choose to take advantage of it. Here's how to win if you lose:

1. Fail quickly. If an idea isn't going to pan out, you might as well figure it out sooner rather than later. It doesn't make sense to invest time and money over twelve months if you could've reached the same conclusion in three weeks.

2. Fail differently each time. Don't repeat mistakes. *Failing loses its value if you don't learn from it.* Each time you fail in a new way, you have the opportunity to improve your approach.

3. After a failure, write down how you can apply that information in the future and next logical steps to ensure getting the most out of it.

Keeping a failure journal records your discoveries and new ideas.

4. Maintain an accurate perspective. *Failure is an undesired result. That's it.* It's not a grading of your intelligence, worth, or future. There's no reason to take it personally. It's simply an idea that didn't work out. Stay detached from your results and forge ahead.

Failure is not the opposite of success, it's part of success. *View each failure as a step in the right direction.*

Naysayers Beware

No matter *where* you are or *who* you are, you will be challenged by negativity. The world is full of naysayers who try to bring you down or make you feel uncomfortable. *If you allow naysayers to discourage you, your life will be much less than you deserve.*

If you're ready to overcome the naysayers in your life, try these strategies:

- *Keep your aspirations to yourself.* Several studies have shown that announcing your goals isn't always a good strategy. The bigger your goals, the more likely you are to receive negative comments. If you're sensitive to the criticism of others, this type of feedback can derail your efforts. Wait to inform everyone after you've accomplished your goal!

- *Avoid taking things personally.* When others are unnecessarily negative, it reveals more about them than it does about you. No one knows enough about your personal business to have an accurate opinion anyway.

- *It's important to keep your vision in mind* and remind yourself of your goals. Be future-focused. Imagine how satisfying it will be when you're proven correct. Nothing is quite as sweet.

- *And as always, consider the source.* Are you trying to launch your own company? Criticism from someone who has always had a corporate job isn't valid. Unless the other person has accomplished your goal, consider the advice worthless. Surround yourself with people who support your efforts and believe in you.

The naysayers will always be around. They aren't going anywhere...and you don't have to go with them. Be confident that you can accomplish anything you set your mind to do.

Oh No, Don't Go Low

Not a week goes by that I don't encounter a new client seeking services that are ultimately a result of low self-esteem. It's not surprising since we live in a world where images of the perfect home, relationships, bodies, and careers are saturating our psyche. If you don't see yourself in those images, it can lead to depression, self-loathing, and poor performance. But you can grow from low to high by giving these recommendations a try:

Surround yourself with positive people and remove the negative people from your life. Spending time with negative people will only reinforce your low opinion of yourself. If you're fortunate enough to have positive influences in your life, listen to them when they say you've done a good job. Avoid ignoring compliments because you feel unworthy. If you were undeserving of the praise, you wouldn't be getting it.

Avoid telling yourself you "should have," "could have," or "would have." If you're constantly telling yourself that, you're focusing on things that have already happened and that you're unable to change. It's better to look to the future and say, "Next time I'll do this," or "I'm going to do that."

Set reasonable expectations. Accept that human beings make mistakes. If you're unwilling to accept anything less than perfection from yourself, you'll feel completely discouraged when you inevitably make a mistake. Remember that every mistake you make is a chance to learn and grow.

Also, recognize and celebrate your accomplishments. Allow yourself to be happy. It's okay to be proud of yourself. Make a list of all your best qualities. Write down your strengths, skills, talents, and positive personality traits. Taking some time to focus on your good qualities can have a very positive effect.

There are many factors that can cause or contribute to low self-esteem. Take the time to figure out how to overcome your low self-esteem so you can start feeling good about yourself. Don't go low, rise high until your thoughts reach the sky!

Fail to Win

It's no secret, but many people are afraid of failing, keeping them in a stagnant state, resulting in unhappiness and restlessness. But in order to win in the game of life, the truth is—sometimes you have to fail.

Some of my most successful coaching clients are individuals who have failed and pursued a new direction, a new way of doing things, or a different way of thinking. Some clients are retired from work but don't want to be retired from life. And others have decided that they want to pursue the things they love that are soul-fulfilling.

The truth is, everyone will fail. And everyone will make mistakes at some point in their career or life. Failure is inevitable—but it is not final. According to an article in *INC* magazine by Abigail Tracy, there are three ways failure brings out the best in people:

- **Failure leads to innovation.** Some of the greatest inventions and discoveries were born out of mistakes—penicillin and the smallpox vaccine are two examples.

- **Failure allows you to identify your weaknesses.** Therefore, you can work on making them strengths and know when you need to seek support.

- **Failure helps you gain perspective.** It humbles you and makes you more realistic about your goals.

Through it all, failure helps you make more informed decisions when you learn from them. Then you can do things better, smarter, and faster! According to Mark Cuban—billionaire investor and star of *Shark Tank,* you can fail many times, but you only have to be right once.

Don't be afraid to try. In the end you will win. Believe the best for your success!

Master Your Thoughts

If you've ever considered a new idea or something different to pursue and immediately begin thinking of the ways it can't be done versus ways it can be done you may have become a victim of limited thinking where you see challenges versus opportunity. Don't be discouraged—the battle of moving forward begins in the mind. Master your thoughts with these three solutions:

First, be aware of the thoughts you are thinking—just because you think it doesn't mean it's true. You don't have to believe everything you think.

Second, watch out for negative themes like worry, dread, or judgment. Most of the things we worry about never happen. Expecting the worst is a set up for failure, and if you constantly think you're not good enough or qualified, you'll never get out of the starting gate. Change and improvement in any area of life is impossible without changing your beliefs. Change a belief and you can change your reality.

And third, practice, practice, practice! Reject the tendency to dwell on the negative. Oftentimes our minds play tricks on us, keeping us distracted and pressing us to engage in the same unproductive behaviors. Remember, you are in control. Fight back! Repeat positive phrases when opposition arises such as, "I am strong enough, smart enough and gifted to handle this new adventure!"

In any situation, you can choose to focus on what is right or what is wrong; either way, you will find evidence to support what you are looking for. Set your mind on success and move forward!

Handle It

While perusing through some of my favorite sources of inspiration, I came across an article by Belle Beth Cooper titled, "Why Our Brains Can't Handle Negative Thoughts." There are two insights I gleaned from the article to manage negativity.

One is a reminder that negative emotions narrow our focus. Negative emotions are one of the most powerful ways to shut our minds off to opportunities or new ideas. A negative thinker sees difficulty in every opportunity. A positive thinker sees an opportunity in every difficulty. Imagine how different your life could be if you looked for solutions in every difficult situation versus doting on the problem.

Another insight is that negativity just doesn't work, literally. Our subconscious brain can't handle it. Scientific studies reveal that our brains can't process negative words. So when we hear a phrase like "Don't smoke" or "Don't touch that," our subconscious skips over these negative words and simply hears "smoke" or "touch that." Our *conscious* mind can obviously process these words, but it's the *subconscious* that makes a lot of our decisions, even though we don't always realize it.

To get around this problem, think of new ways to phrase things. Replace negative words with positivity or affirmations. Rather than saying "Don't smoke," you can say, "Be smoke free." Instead of saying to your child, "Don't throw that rock," you should say "Put down the rock." Instead of telling yourself what *not to do* in social situations, try focusing on what *to do*.

What you think you will attract. Think on purpose!

Get Started

Twelve frogs are sitting on a log along the river. Seven decide to jump in...how many are still sitting on the log? Did you say five or twelve? The answer is all of them—twelve. Even though seven *decided* to jump into the river, they didn't take action and do it. There's a big difference in *doing* versus *deciding*.

Just as in life, we all make decisions, but if we don't act, we aren't going anywhere. Nothing changes, and we're still sitting on the log.

If you want to excel, it takes action. You don't have to be great to get started, but you have to get started to be great. So what's holding you back from achieving more, doing more, being more?

Be honest with yourself and find a way to end the delay. Here's my three-step process:

1. **Make a plan.** Determine what you want to accomplish and identify two tasks that will move you forward.

2. **Get support.** Ask someone to keep you accountable to your goals.

3. **Take it one step at a time.** The secret to getting ahead is getting started. Soon you'll look back and wonder what took you so long.

In all, push yourself because no one else is going to do it for you. You can achieve what you *believe* and *work for!*

Strategies to Strengthen Your Self-Esteem

Our view of ourselves can dictate the course our entire lives. *How we see ourselves can be self-fulfilling prophecies.* For example, if we see ourselves as underserving, there is only a small chance that we will end up attaining our desires.

Furthermore, how we view ourselves can affect our relationships with others, and we may find ourselves continually in unsatisfying relationships that are either abusive or lacking in some fundamental way.

Feelings of nervousness, anxiety, and a pervasive sense of our own inadequacy are all things that can come along with having low self-esteem. Just as having a weak self-esteem lends itself to all of the issues mentioned, *strengthening your self-esteem can lead to the positive outcomes you desire.*

To strengthen your self-esteem, put unhappy feelings behind you, and start living the life you were meant to live.

- **Turn negative beliefs upside down.** Negative beliefs that you're not good enough have got to go! *Start by writing down the things that you can do well and examples of things that you've been successful at in the past.* You may not feel a difference right away, however, writing down these facts helps to challenge the assumptions that your negative beliefs are currently based on. Over time, you may notice that you're feeling more confident and that your self-esteem is slowly being strengthened.

- **Put your needs first**. This doesn't mean that you have to be selfish. It's more about not putting your own needs aside to make others happy before you make yourself happy. Why should everyone else be happy but you? That doesn't seem very fair, now does it? There's nothing wrong with wanting to make others happy. In fact, this is a very nice thing, yet doing this at the expense of your own happiness is a recipe for dissatisfaction and resentment in the long run. *When you practice making yourself and others happy, everyone around you will thank you for it, as you'll be much more pleasant company when you're happy too.*

- **Find friends who support your self-esteem.** Maybe the current crowd you hang out with continually cuts you down and finds fault in what you do. Perhaps you already have friends who are there to pick you up when you fall down. If the people you surround yourself with are like the latter, then that's great! If not, why waste time hanging out with people who make you feel badly, when there are many people out there who want to support you and make you feel better about yourself? These are called true friends. Finding them is not always easy, it may not happen overnight, but that's okay. *Remember what you deserve, and find people who see you in a positive light as well.*

By taking these steps, you'll be going a long way toward strengthening your self-esteem and will be well on the road toward feeling happy and confident in yourself.

You're in Charge

Would you say that you are the type of person who is easily influenced by others? Do you find yourself agreeing just to keep the peace or to be part of the group? If so, this means that you are not really being true to yourself. You are not allowing your personality, thoughts, and feelings to emerge.

It takes confidence to be in opposition. It is much easier to stay silent or just nod your head in agreement. It takes guts to speak out politely, but when you do, you will feel so proud of yourself for doing so.

By airing your views to your friends and family, they may see you in a different light. They might not even agree or understand your point of view, but that's okay.

While it is easy to allow others to influence your life, you should not let anyone do this all the time. To get out of this scenario, you want to surround yourself with people who are open to everyone just being themselves. This might be dressing the way you want to, having different views or only eating specific foods. No one should judge you for your actions. They should just appreciate that your actions are an extension of the real you.

So if you are feeling as though you are not living the life you were meant to live, remember that you're in charge of you. Stand up for yourself. Choose your own path and be prepared to accept any consequence, good or bad. You can be the person you truly want to be by taking action, starting today.

You were born to *thrive* not just survive.

Who Are They?

My career is purposed to support individuals who seek to gain more success with their professional careers. Some are looking to advance to the next level. Others desire a promotion in their current workplace. And some are opting for an entirely new career that better aligns with their life passion. Often the challenge they face has nothing to do with their skills. The challenge is in their relationship with others.

What will *they* say? What will *they* think? What if *they* don't support me? Here's the thing, until you can ignore ignorance, neglect negativity, and disregard disrespect, you aren't ready for the next step. A new level brings new devils, new attacks, and even setbacks. To stay engaged enough to make the change, there are three types of people who can positivity influence your journey.

One type is decision makers who can provide you with direct leads, direct work, or bridge you to the contacts who can. The second type of person to have in your network are those who are information sources. They provide valuable knowledge of companies, industries and trends, and people you need to know. The third type are cheerleaders who provide references, testimonials, and they'll vouch for you. They are your personal board of directors. They are vested in your success and are also a source of encouragement.

In all, don't focus on the naysayers. Focus on people who love you and support you because *they* are the ones who matter.

Accept Yourself

Have you ever thought, *Oh no, I can't do that* or *I'm not smart enough* or *that's only for those other kinds of people* when pursuing a promotion or other goal in life? If you answered yes, you're not alone. It's common for people to feel unhappy with who they are, what they've attained in life, or which path they're taking. And that's because we are all human. Sure there will be days when your best doesn't seem good enough to you, but what if your best is really just fine?

To get out of that stinking thinking, you've got to come to terms with your true self and acknowledge the awesome person you really are. No one else has your individual talents. No one else could ever take your unique place in this world.

To achieve contentment with the skin you're in:

Know that you are special. Look at the person you are as a beautiful creation. *You weren't made this way by mistake.* Your beliefs, likes, and dislikes are all part of your magnificent design. Often times, people get stuck because they may feel that someone else's situation is better than theirs because they have more, seem to be happier, or appear better off. But consider your gifts and opportunities; there are people who need a job like the one you may be complaining about. Always count your blessing—not your burdens.

Review your accomplishments. Whether you accomplished a stronger bond with your parents or completed a project that won your workplace a new contract, those took place because of who you are. You did it with your own strength, abilities, and sensibilities.

Avoid underestimating yourself. Is it possible that you don't have what you want because you haven't really tried to get it? Instead of wishing you had what somebody else has, why not put some thought into how you can achieve it for yourself. Make a detailed plan of achievable steps to get what you want.

You were uniquely created with the talents and skills to have a fulfilling life. Keep in mind—what you deny or ignore, you delay. What you accept and face, you conquer!

Do Over!

Ezra Harris, a retired deputy sheriff, was asked to sing the national anthem for a police event. However, a few words in it was clearly noticeable that Ezra either didn't know or forgot the words and some notes. To add to the misery he was already feeling, the local event was captured on video and circulated on the internet garnering millions of views of his epic fail.

However, Ezra Harris had a chance for a do over when the producers of *Good Morning America* contacted him, arranged for singing lessons and gave him a chance to sing with the support of a gospel choir. After the redeeming performance, Ezra said it felt wonderful to be able to reinvent himself.

In our life's journey, we have all had moments we wish we could do over. We've either said or done something we wish we could take back and erase or make whole. The following are my three tips if you've suffered this kind of failure:

- **Forgive yourself.** Pain is the fist that knocks you down, but forgiveness is the hand that helps you get up again. We all make mistakes. Ignore your inner critic and move on. Let the past be the past.

- **Get support.** Confide in individuals who can help you build in the area of your failure and provide guidance to help you rebound and get past the hurt, embarrassment, discomfort, or shame.

- **Grow.** When you make a mistake, it is an opportunity to learn and begin again. If you're not making mistakes, you aren't living; mistakes are part of life.

Life is a journey not a destination. It's not over until it's over! Get up and keep pushing!

Problem Solving

A barrier to some peoples' success isn't that they don't have the right resources or contacts or skills. The challenge lies in their ability to solve problems. For some it is difficult to commit to a task or goal because of the fear of making the wrong decision.

There is no single way to solve problems or magic formula to ensure you make the right decision all the time, but these four tips can help you become more effective in dealing with situations and circumstances that can derail your progress.

Identify the problem. Many people usually try to avoid, procrastinate, and ignore facing difficulties. Be brave; identify what went wrong. What are the symptoms and the impact on your career and your life? Then, write it down. Develop a list so you know what you're working with you to begin the process of resolving the problems.

Next, **define the problem.** Albert Einstein said, "If I had sixty minutes to solve a problem, I'd spend fifty-five minutes defining it and five minutes solving it." This is the key to your success with problem-solving efforts.

Another tip is to **find the challenges.** An obstacle is usually in the way we look at problems. Find the benefits or opportunities in a problem. For example, if your current problem is not getting along with colleagues, it is an opportunity to improve your communication skills and resolve conflicts with your coworkers.

And **generate different actions or solutions** for your problems. The biggest mistake people usually make is that they tend to think of the same old ways of dealing with difficulties. Think in a new way by brainstorming. Ask "what if". Try to come up with many different solutions to increase the likelihood for solving your problem.

And remember this, life is a journey with problems to solve and lessons to learn—but most of all, experiences to enjoy!

Don't Fit In and Win

In the 1990s, I accidentally on purpose did something that changed my life. Professional "appropriate business attire" in those days consisted of black, navy blue, and drab grey suits. At first I thought it was fun to be dressed like everyone else…to fit in. But I soon grew tired of that boring wardrobe. So one day I wore a red suit. I had no idea the impact that decision would have on my career. Everyone, and I mean everyone, stopped and stared. Some even glared. I became known as "the lady with the red suit." People began to pay attention to me. My lack of conformity led to a change in perceptions and the direction of my next steps throughout the organization.

In fact, unbeknown to me at that time, Harvard researchers conducted a number of experiments to see if violating the dress code could make people seem more prestigious. And it's true. The results revealed that being different can get you noticed.

So if you're tired of fitting in, stand out so you can win! Do this by taking risks. For example, be the first to try a new time management app and share your success with others in your department. Consider creative ways to contribute to your team. Even if your idea doesn't work out, your boss will recognize that you are thinking differently to support the bottom line, and most likely you'll be encouraged to keep trying because innovative thinkers are valuable team members.

If you want to stand out from the crowd, give people a reason *not* to forget you. You'll increase your chances of developing a rewarding career and leading a more meaningful life.

The Clothing Connection

I'm sometimes asked, "Do clothes really make the person?" My answer is yes! The way you dress says a lot about you. You may rarely think about it, but what you're wearing today might have been a direct expression of how you felt when you selected the outfit this morning. Maybe you didn't care or were feeling down when you were getting dressed. But on a day you *do* care or you have something special to dress up for, you take extra time to look your best.

Your clothing reflects your feelings. And the research supports it. Professor Karen Pine of the University of Hertfordshire researched how a person's attire affects confidence. She had some of her students put on Superman T-shirts and then take a survey about how they felt about themselves. Those wearing the Superman shirts reported they were more likeable and even physically stronger than those who weren't wearing the Superman shirts.

Think about it this way. If you've ever been in the hospital, as soon as you put on that baggy hospital gown, you feel vulnerable, unsure of yourself, and defenseless. Your physical symptoms may even worsen.

In contrast, when you dress up to go to a wedding or fancy dinner, you feel elegant and amazing. For most of us, putting on our "Sunday best" brings out our best manners and makes us feel confident about our looks.

If you find yourself in a somber mood, be aware of your gear! There is a mood connection to our clothing selection. Go through your closet today and donate outfits that seem to bring you down. Who knows, those same clothes might lift the spirits of someone else!

The better you think you look, the better you feel about yourself. When you have a wardrobe that's appealing to you, you'll live a happier, more confident life.

Losing

One day a young football player emphatically made comments at the end of a game, that were perceived negatively and ended up putting him on the path to infamy. I'm not a football fan or follower, but I couldn't escape the swirl of news stories talking about the player with a head full of dreadlocks who was angry and screaming in the camera. That day we all learned the name Richard Sherman.

Richard Sherman wasn't a player that coaches and professors pushed through college for the sake of the game. Sherman graduated with a 3.7 GPA from Stanford University, stayed to get his master's degree, and was raised by both parents who are still married. He is a philanthropist, a youth volunteer, and a dedicated professional who spends weekends studying versus hanging out where most men his age are found.

Sherman may have lost his cool, but he gained the spotlight that now affords him many lucrative opportunities. Here are some of my favorite sayings about losing that will help you win in the end:

1. There are some people you have to lose in order to find yourself.

2. You never lose by loving. You always lose by holding back.

3. It's the strength to stand up after a loss that is sometimes more valuable than winning.

4. Winning or losing achieves the same result—change.

5. It's better to lose than to never have had to lose.

6. The heartbreak of losing fades over time; however, the burden of quitting lasts forever.

In life, there will be times when we lose control, opportunities, and friends. Winning isn't everything. Some of our greatest achievements can happen when we lose. Don't be afraid to lose in order to gain!

Stretch

They say you should always practice what you preach. In other words, take your own medicine. And that's what I've had to do. After being very, very thin for most of my life, it happened. The 40s came and so did the weight, so I started exercising. The first few days I couldn't get beyond the first ten minutes of the abs workout before falling faint on the floor. It was painful. I was taking Advil every evening just to lift my legs onto the bed. But I knew I had to stretch beyond what my body was saying to hear what my mind was saying, *YOU CAN DO IT!* In time, I've gotten better and now exercise for thirty minutes.

The key was not giving up. And when I felt weak, I told myself, *KEEP GOING!* It's the same with everything in life. No matter how difficult the task or situation, you must press your way through. At first it may be painful and you will want to throw in the towel, but always remember why you started to help stay focused.

Your outcome and results will only change if you first change what precedes that—your beliefs, thoughts, feelings, and your actions!

I'm still exercising and the results are showing. But my greatest reward is how much better I feel as I continue making my way through.

You are confined only by the walls you build yourself. Your life only gets better when you do. Work on yourself and the rest will follow.

Lessons of Depression

Depression is known as a disease that cripples its victims, leaving them barely able to function. Daniel Grant not only battled depression but he won. Daniel is the author of *The War on Self,* sharing what he learned as an overcomer. These lessons of depression can help anyone succeed in anything. Here are a few:

Lesson 1. It does get better; it won't feel like it will, but it will. Keep going!

Lesson 2. The mistakes you make now are okay. Depression can lock you into a world where nothing goes your way and you feel stuck. Continue working on yourself and your issues anyway. You'll build momentum to grow.

Lesson 3. You will always be struggling with something— accept that. There will be trials and tribulations as long as you're breathing. It's the cycle of life.

Lesson 4. Believe in *you*. Putting your faith in other people or a company or a boss can be devastating if (and when) they let you down. To make progress and do better—trust yourself.

Remember these lessons to overcome depression and increase opportunities for success in life!

PART VI

GOALS AND THE FUTURE

Goals on Fire

Do you struggle to reach your goals? If you said yes, you're not alone. Science says that 92% of people don't achieve their goals. One thing that makes goals so difficult to achieve is how hard it is to stay focused enough to keep working toward them. Despite our best intentions and efforts, it can be quite daunting to stay on track!

There are a few simple strategies that you can implement to help you stay focused and make significant progress. Try these:

- **Narrow your list.** Instead of trying to focus on too many goals, narrow it down to one to three major goals that you hope to achieve within the year. This ensures that you aren't spreading yourself too thin and, as a result, losing your motivation.

- **Break down each of your major goals.** How do you eat an elephant? One bite at a time. You'll feel less overwhelmed when you break up a large goal into a series of smaller steps, each with specific, achievable tasks. This makes reaching your ultimate goal that much easier.

- **Get a goal buddy!** This person can encourage you when obstacles arise and celebrate your successes with you along the way.

- **Record and document your process.** Start a journal and write about your experience as you pursue your goal. Writing down your thoughts is a great way to maintain your motivation to the end.

- **Create a goal board.** This is a visual reminder of why you created a particular goal in the first place. It makes it easier to visualize how you'll feel once your goal is complete. In effect, it gets your subconscious mind "on board" with your plan to reach your goal.

It takes hard work and consistent effort to achieve major goals. Use these tips to maintain your passion and make your dreams come true!

Retire?

Rashard Mendenhall, a football running back, announced that he was retiring after only six seasons in the NFL—walking away from the opportunity to earn millions of dollars. Rashard wrote in a post titled "Why I Retired At 26," that he didn't think walking away was that big of a deal. He wrote, "Football was pretty cool, but I don't want to play anymore." Rashard is doing what most people only imagine. He is walking away from a career—that most people would die to have—to live his dream.

Of course his decision was met with shock, bewilderment, and lots of questions. When asked what he would do, Rashard said, "I will LIVE! I plan to live in a way that I never have before, and that is freely, able to fully be me, without the expectation of representing any league, club, shield or city. I do have a plan going forward, but I will admit that I do not know how things will totally shape out. That is the beauty of it! I want to travel the world and write!"

When you follow your passion, you may not have all the answers, you may not even know where to start; but what you do know is that you have to do something different. Many people have started with much less and achieved remarkable success. The only difference between them and others is that they believed in themselves and were willing to risk losing in order to gain in the future.

Decide that you want it more than you're afraid of it. If you want more out of life, don't let the fear of failure, the unknown, or opinions of others suffocate your dreams and desires. The only person who will suffer from the inaction is you. Don't wait for the perfect moment. *Make* the moment! Miracles happen every day!

You are divinely designed to succeed. You were made for excellence! Follow your heart, but don't forget to take your head with you.

See It, Achieve It

As the daughter-in-law of a carpenter, I was privileged to be able to watch Papa build bookshelves, benches, tables, and chair sets. The process he used in creating his masterpieces all started with a vision of the final project.

As a coach, I challenge clients to do the same. You can reach your goals by creating a vision board for your life. Using poster board, cardboard, a notebook, or even a spare wall, you can create a vision board that works for you. If you want to make changes in the new year, get started today.

First, determine your goals for the year. Perhaps your goals are a fit body, a new car, and a vacation to Hawaii. It's up to you. Make your vision so clear that your fears become irrelevant.

Next, select images that symbolize the future you'd like to achieve. Find pictures that best represent the goals you wish to achieve using magazines, newspapers, or content from the internet. If you're striving for a new car, find the exact model and color.

Then, choose the best words to go on your vision board, like "Mustang" or "Honolulu." Collect and post the words that express how you'll feel when the goal is achieved: "Thrilled," "Grateful," "Accomplished." Also, choose the qualities will you need to achieve these goals like "Committed" and "Powerful."

Now you're ready to create your board. Get out your scissors, glue, and tape to mount the words and photos onto your board.

To stay engaged, keep your vision board where you see it at least twice each day. Spending a few minutes each morning viewing your vision board will set the tone for the rest of your day. Be sure to take your time and visualize having those things in your life.

Turn "I wish" into "I will." See it. Believe it. Achieve it!

C Your Way to Success

There's no secret formula to success, but there are things successful people do to reach their goals. Whether you define success in terms of money, happiness, fame, or family, achieving success takes effort. Aristotle said we are what we repeatedly do. Excellence is not an act, but a habit.

The first *C* of success is **CONSISTENCY.** Consistency is the key that unlocks the door to success. It's the small efforts repeated day in and day out that lead you to accomplishing your goals. Understand that consistency is essential—not optional, nothing is achieved without it. Be consistent in your approach, your attitude, communications, and actions.

The second *C* is **COMMITMENT.** Be passionate about the goals you are pursuing and the life you are living. You must be a self-motivator and self-generator. Don't sit around and wait for someone to give you an opportunity. Be committed to generating opportunities for yourself. This involves meeting new people, being open to new ideas, and contributing to the well-being of others.

And the third *C* is **CONFIDENCE.** Encouragement must come from within. If no one else celebrates you, learn to celebrate yourself. When no one else compliments you, compliment yourself. It's not up to other people to keep you encouraged. That's *your* job. Everything else is bonus.

Be Consistent, Committed, and Confident—and *C* your way to success!

Identify Theft

In recent times, we have learned of security breaches at major retailers, hacks breaking into company databases and many other scams. In the age of the internet, it's become a major challenge for companies to keep our information secure. These actions can lead to theft of our personal information.

Hopefully you haven't been a victim and were not robbed of your finances; but if you're not careful, you can be robbed of treasures that are even more valuable…like your peace, comfort, or your time.

Don't let negativity rob you of opportunity. Beginning now, make goals that will move you. Be specific and commit to a date to finish what you start. Begin by writing down your goals, then share with someone you trust, and finally get going one step at a time.

Should fear creep into the scene, don't despair—declare that you are better, stronger, and capable of doing all things.

Rules Are Cool

If you find yourself going over and over and over many of your decisions, doubting yourself, I've got a solution for you.

You can experience a *profound freedom from doubt by implementing a set of rules that you've chosen for yourself. Rules provide the framework for having a more productive and stress-free life.*

Develop your own set of rules for each aspect of your life. Here's how:

- **Make a list of your most important goals.** Include those related to your finances, health, family, and personal accomplishments. *If you know your goals, you can develop rules that support them.*

- **Set rules by understanding your values.** The rules will drive your behavior and you'll be much happier and more successful.

- **Set rules by identifying time wasters, obstacles, and your weaknesses.** Eliminate or minimize those challenges.

- **And set rules by looking at the example you are setting for others.** How other people respond to you reflects your rules.

Most of us are striving for a greater degree of freedom, and rules seem like a limit to freedom. *However, you will free up a lot of mental resources when you make important decisions beforehand.* If your rule is to exercise every day, then you will avoid spending twenty minutes deciding whether or not to exercise. You just do it.

Take time to make your own set of rules. The number doesn't matter. Start with a couple and add more as you see fit. Make rules for yourself to set yourself free.

Think then Do

Every great achievement starts in the mind, spurring us to action. Successful people THINK every day the following thoughts that lead to remarkable results for the future:

- THINK, *I can't do everything today, but I can take one small step.* You have plans. You have goals. You have ideas. But you have nothing until you actually *do* something. Pick one plan, one goal, or one idea, then take a step toward success.

- THINK, *I'll do it!* Volunteer for a new work assignment. Stepping up and doing more creates an opportunity to learn, to impress, to gain skills, to build new relationships, to do something that you would otherwise never have been able to do. *Success is based on action,* so the more you volunteer, the more you get to act, and the more opportunities you create.

- THINK, *No one else will do it, so I will.* The easiest way to be different is to do what others are unwilling to do. Pick one thing other people won't do. It can be simple. It can be small. Then do it and keep going. After a week, you'll be uncommon. After a month, you'll be special. After a year, you'll be incredible, and you definitely won't be like anyone else.

You can achieve greater things in life by taking small steps, volunteering, and doing what others won't. Be remarkable! Be determined! Think, then do! Be you!

From Average to Awesome

Few things in life are constant. *Small, constant changes are happening all the time.* This is true even while driving in a seemingly straight line down the highway. You're constantly making course corrections to prevent your car from crossing over the lines.

The quality of your life is no different. *Small corrections, applied consistently, can take your life in a vastly different direction.* Are you choosing the direction of your life? Or are you living your life by default and simply taking whatever life throws your way?

Think about it this way, if you lived yesterday over and over for the next ten years, where would you land?

The things you do, or fail to do, each day determine your destiny. Design a productive day in these four ways and create your exciting future:

1. **Exercise.** A little bit of exercise can go a long way if performed religiously. There's no reason to train as if you're fighting to be in the next *Rocky* movie. Gently pushing yourself a tiny bit more each week is more than enough.

2. **Communicate with those who matter.** Relationships crumble a little at time. Talk to the important people in your life each day and have a meaningful chat. Even a short text message can be better than nothing.

3. **Develop habits to enhance your employment.** Make a list of things you could do each day at work to ensure your success long-term. It might

involve speaking each day with the employees who report to you. Or maybe you need to ensure your work is done on time consistently. All things matter!

4. **Remember your goals.** If you've always wanted to learn to speak Spanish, set aside fifteen minutes each day and get started. Or if you've desired to start your own business, spend thirty minutes listening to podcasts related to your interest instead of watching television.

The key is to get ready for where you're going and not for where you were! Move from average to awesome by creating a day that will ensure a positive, happy, and rewarding future if you repeat it over the long haul.

You Can Make It!

To live a successful life takes courage, determination, energy, and focus. It's like a marriage or any relationship—you've got to work at it, nurture it, and feed it positivity in order to maintain and gain. Neila Rey offers some advice on how to reach your goals and not give up. How can you achieve what you believe:

1. **Take a shot.** Every day holds a new opportunity. Today is a good day to look for it.

2. **Be realistic.** Don't set yourself up for failure from the beginning. Be true to what you can do. Remember, slow progress is still progress.

3. **Stay strong.** You have it in you, just stay with it. It *will* get better.

4. **Keep focusing on the target.** If you're not seeing change, then shake things up. Try a new approach to reach the target.

5. **Persist.** Things always seem to get worse before they get better; your job is to keep moving forward.

6. **Don't doubt.** If you wonder, *Is it worth it?* The answer is always YES!

7. **Be wary of interruptions.** Before you can reach your goal, there are always distractions and temptations to go back and do what you are comfortable with. Don't give up; you're closer than you think.

You can make it! And if all else fails, just FAITH it!

Shift into High Gear

Have you been through some difficult challenges that have drained or destroyed your confidence? Maybe it was a job loss or failed relationship? If you are you unsure of how to pick up the pieces and go about believing in yourself again, consider these tips to **shift your confidence levels into high gear:**

Shift to reconnect with *you*. Practice self-reflection to rediscover your strengths. Recognize the awesomeness of you by acknowledging your past accomplishments.

Shift by acknowledging the fantastic people you have in your life. Think of your friends and the close relationships you enjoy with your family members. Think of the associations you have with coworkers you respect and admire. Your confidence will be lifted by thoughts of the incredible people in your circle.

Shift to embrace challenges. Tell yourself, *I may not succeed but, I will definitely give it my all.* And tackle opportunities that will help you grow.

Regaining confidence can be tough, especially when you've been emotionally hurt or professionally scarred. Keep in mind that failure is not final and success is not a destination—it's a journey. You can always begin again. Shift into high gear and focus on your SUCCESS!

Note to Self

A popular coaching exercise to reveal your authenticity and identify your strengths and weaknesses is to write a letter to your younger self. I completed this exercise by writing a note to my 16-year-old self. It was powerful and revealing. Each time I repeat the exercise, I often discover something different about myself.

Sometimes I'm laughing, *What in the world made me like that guy Robert?* And other times I'm crying, *What was that hairdo all about?! Why did I think I could start a trend with stars and stripes? Somebody please burn those images...*

The flip of that exercise is to write to your older self to identify your goals and dreams and vision for your future. In my letter to my 80-year-old self I imagined what I would say to myself. I envisioned what I would accomplish, and gave myself a pat on the back. The contents of that letter drives me everyday. It's the fuel that lights my journey.

Here's *your* homework. Write a letter to your 16-year-old self. Start by looking through old photo albums and scrapbooks; call your childhood friends or spend time reminiscing about events that impacted your life the most. Take a trip down memory lane and tell yourself how proud you are that you made it.

Or you can begin a journey into the future. Write a letter to your 80-year-old self. This is an exercise of encouragement, motivation, and celebration. Mine read something like this: Adrean, you made it. You didn't give up even though other people in your same situation would have quit. You achieved what you set out to do. Congratulations, your future.

Believe the best for your future!

Now not Later

In 2007, Morgan Freeman starred in a movie titled, *The Bucket List*. Freeman's character was Carter, a mechanic, and Jack Nicholson played a billionaire named Edward. They shared a hospital room because of terminal cancer, and Edward found Carter's "bucket list." Then they decided to do all the things they had ever wanted to do before each "kicked the bucket." In the process, both of them ultimately found joy in life.

I want to encourage you to pursue your goals to realize joy *now,* not *later.* Don't wait for the cancers of life to force your hand. Like Edward and Carter, some of us have put our dreams, hopes, and aspirations on hold. Move forward toward your destiny. Don't let other illnesses of life discourage you from achieving the best that life has to offer.

During a coaching seminar, someone mentioned that she thought she was too old to be influential and pursue her dreams. I reminded her of the story of Ruth and her mother-in-law, Naomi. Naomi guided and encouraged Ruth with her wisdom, which led them both to fulfilling their destiny. Someone else said, "I don't have the skills." My response, "Then get the skills. There is no reason you shouldn't be pursuing the things in life that God has purposed for you."

In the movie, Edward says to Carter, *"I envy people who have faith, I just can't get my head around it."* To which Carter replies, *"Maybe because your head's in the way."* I encourage you, don't let your head get in the way! Do it *now!*

Get started creating your own bucket list. It will keep you inspired, focused, and moving forward.

Blessings Overflow

Are you the type of person who likes to count your blessings? If so, this means that you have learned what it means to be grateful for certain things in your life. These can be physical assets like owning your own home, or on a more personal level, by being grateful for someone in your life.

The concept of being grateful for what you have can be difficult for some people to understand. Instead of focusing on what they have, many people find it easier to be constantly thinking about what they *don't* have.

Think about this for a moment. Do you really have to be wealthy to feel as though you are? Will having a million dollars in the bank automatically make you happy? The answer to both of these questions is no. Money doesn't buy you happiness, and you don't need physical wealth to feel wealthy.

Wealth can be compared to having abundance and gratitude in your life. If you are surrounded by people who love and respect you, you will instantly feel treasured in return. A person who has just undergone lifesaving surgery can feel extremely grateful to be alive. Even though the person may be faced with months of rehab and physiotherapy.

When you think about what you have to be grateful for, you should look further than just physical things. There is more to life than money and owning all the latest and greatest tech items on the market. Being grateful for your life consists of understanding what you have gone through to get to where you are today. This includes your struggles and fears as well as your successes and failures.

Just Two Will Do

If you want to stay on track of achieving your goals, forget about reading long books or downloading a slew of podcasts. *You might be surprised at how much you can benefit from asking yourself just two questions!* Your answers will help determine if you're moving in the right direction and enable you to make an action plan that will get you there in record time.

Ask yourself, *If an invisible person followed me around all day, what would the person see?* Would the person see you wasting a lot of time, working on your goals, or just going through the motions? Our lives are largely the result of the actions we take each day. Are you taking actions that move you forward to the future you desire? Or are you engaged in time-wasting, worthless activity?

Ask yourself, *If I lived that average day, every day for the next five years, what is the logical outcome?* Now compare that conclusion with the life you'd like to have. How close are they?

- Are you likely to end up where you want to be financially?

- Are you likely to have the body you want? Are you eating nutritiously and exercising regularly?

- Are you likely to be enjoying the type of relationships you desire?

- Are you likely to be advancing in the career you seek? For example, based on your performance over the last year, do you think it's probable that you'll get that manager position anytime soon?

- Are you any closer to having that small business running profitably?

People largely fail to end up where they wish to be for two reasons: 1. They have no idea where they're going; and 2. they don't do the things each day that will create the life they want. Regardless of what any expert tells you, you can't wish your way to success. Success is the result of making positive decisions and taking actions that reflect those decisions.

What you do on a consistent basis is what determines the results you get. It doesn't take a lot to be very successful, but it does take consistency.

Break the Old and Welcome the New

It's well known that the only constant in life is change. But change is hard for most people. The truth is, 95 percent of our behaviors are habitual, which means only 5 percent of our choices are consciously self-selected. But don't despair. There are ways you can make changes that are remarkably powerful and enduring.

The following are six strategies you can use to be more efficient when you choose *change for the better:*

1. To make a change that lasts, *be specific.* Instead of saying. "I'll exercise regularly." Say instead, "I'm committed to doing a cardiovascular workout Monday, Wednesday, and Friday at 6 a.m., for 30 minutes."

2. *Take on one new challenge at a time.* Although computers can run several programs simultaneously, human beings operate best when we take on one thing at a time, sequentially. Take your time and you'll be fine.

3. *Don't overdo it.* The most obvious mistake we make when we try to change is that we bite off more than we can chew. Find a middle ground— push yourself hard enough that you get some real gain, but not too much that you find yourself unwilling to stay at it.

4. Be in it to win in by *avoiding temptations.* Learn to ignore distractions and think on purpose to resist habitual behavior.

5. *Abolish competing commitments.* We all derive a sense of comfort and safety from doing what we've always done. To make the change you really want, design a practice to get the outcome you desire to minimize old habits that compete with your new objectives.

6. In all that you do, *keep the faith.* The average person launches a change effort six separate times

before it finally takes hold. Don't be dismayed
if you're delayed. Stay focused on your success.

Break the mold of the old and welcome change in your life
for more joy, energy, and abundance!

The Fight for Life

If you're a success seeker you've probably set some pretty
enormous goals for your life. They may include ambitions that
could take you five or ten years or sometimes even longer to
make the goals become realities. This necessitates a ton of willpower and persistence and determination.

The big questions for most people—and I've battled with
these myself many times—are: *How do I keep that fighting spirit
alive to reach my goal? How do I keep getting up every day, exud-
ing all my energy toward taking one step closer to my goal, when
some days it feels like I'm going in reverse?*

There are a number of ways and strategies to answer, but
what's been most helpful for me is to understand the driving
force or the reason why I set the goal in the first place.

The big goal I've been working on is to build my own successful company. I've made some excellent progress over the
past five years, which has been very, very exciting. However,
there were many days when that fighting spirit was challenged,
when I felt like it would be a lot easier if I just went back and
picked up a 9 to 5 job.

On those days, it's my "reason why" that kicked in. The
reason why was much bigger and much more important to me
than any pain or suffering or frustration I was feeling in any
given moment. When I started focusing on the reason why I

was building this business in the first place, I was immediately rejuvenated with new energy and a new fighting spirit to keep going, even on those dark days when I didn't really feel like it was worth the effort anymore.

That's the key. What is your reason why? What's your driving force? As you glance into the future and look at what you're working on right now, come back to the present moment and remember your reason why—it will immediately generate the fighting spirit you need, anytime you need it.

Good luck with your goals.

Ain't No Bones about It

It's been said that to succeed in life you need three bones: a wishbone, backbone, and a funny bone. A *wishbone* symbolizing hope. It gives you something to look forward to. Something to hold on to. Something to help you focus on in the future to make your dreams come true.

To succeed in life you need a *backbone,* which represents strength. A person with a strong backbone has guts; they are the glue that holds things together. They mend relationships. They are consulted on important issues. They get the job done.

And to succeed, you also need a *funny bone.* To be able to find joy and laughter in everyday living is a blessing.

Live, love, and laugh. You only live once, but if you do it right, once is enough. And there ain't no bones about it!

A Better Future

As we age, there is a natural yearning and pulling that makes us reflect on the past and seek ways to have a better future—one that is more connected with our spirit versus the tangible things of life. If you seek to have greater awareness and inner peace, consider these three approaches to spiritual wellness:

- **Meditate.** Meditation is the perfect medium for connecting to your inner self. It is important to maintain that connection so you remain in tune with your spiritual beliefs. It's also a great way to help focus on the present. Focusing on the present also keeps you from worrying about the future.

- **Make value-guided decisions.** Living a life in tune with your values is the best way to be true to yourself. In turn, this trueness allows your spiritual life to flourish. What do you value? Is it honesty and truth? Is it charity? Those decisions should sit well within spirit.

- **Connect with the meaning of situations** as an approach to gain greater spiritual wellness. *Everything happens for a reason!* As cliché as it is, it's the most accurate explanation for life. What you do with the information presented is another matter.

It's important to understand that not everything is built in your favor; but understanding why things happen helps in your journey to truly accept yourself.

Stay connected with who you are on the inside and you are sure to gain the joyful peace of spiritual wellness. Life is *all* about the journey—not the destination. Live! Learn! Love!

Be a Better You!

During a conference, I shared information on the topic "Getting to know you." The fact is, most people know more about others than they know about themselves. But yet they want to change their personality for the traits they *do* recognize. If you want to make some adjustments to your personality and attract more success, happiness, and opportunities, apply these strategies to sway your personality traits in a direction you desire:

- **Realize how your life experiences influence you.** Graduating from college, finding a job, getting married, having children—all those events morph your personality so you can fit into your chosen life. Embrace the newness of you.

- **To build stronger relationships, work on being more agreeable.** Consider the needs of others before your own and step up to being a helpful, giving individual. Your relationships will bloom and prosper—and so will you.

- **The more focused and conscientious you are about changing, the more you'll change.** Set specific, personal goals in the areas where you wish to grow. Use sticky notes for reminders, and reward yourself for progress made.

- **Learn to be your own cheerleader.** Say positive things about yourself. Each morning I tell myself, *I am smart. I am loved, and I can do what I need to do to have a productive day.* Pump yourself up and own your power!

Become a better you and live on purpose!

The Past Should Not Last

Sometimes we face challenges that leave us feeling stuck, looking back wistfully to earlier years and wishing things could have remained "that way." Maybe you lost a meaningful relationship or a job that has caused you to dwell on the past. Memories are good, but when they prevent you from moving forward and enjoying a more fulfilling life, it's time to make a change.

Here's how you know when you're living in the past:

- **Every day you think about how your life used to be.** Maybe you call it "nostalgia" or simple yearnings for what your life was like before.

- **You sleep a lot...dreaming about earlier years.** Those dreams become fantasies and you look forward to them.

- **You spend a lot of time on the computer,** trying to keep busy so you don't have to think about how your life has changed.

- **Maybe you use other methods to "escape" from reality** like reading, cleaning, or even drinking alcohol. You are constantly in motion, doing something so you don't have to face life as it is now.

- **Or if you're in denial about your current living situation,** you're probably living in the past. It's hard to accept that you no longer have a partner or the same job but, *it's time to start living in the here and now.*

Now that you recognize you may be living in the past:

1. Openly acknowledge to yourself what you've been doing so you can heal.

2. Decide what you must do to shift into the present—and actively pursue it.

3. Take care of yourself physically and mentally.

4. Don't waste another moment. *Practice gratitude* for each new day.

Living in the past robs you of the life you truly deserve. It's never too late to begin again and enjoy every today!

Mind Power

As I work with career reinventors and individuals who want to transition into new life experiences, I've come to realize a very important fact: the greatest barriers to success aren't other people, lack of money, the wrong location, or not having the right connections—*the greatest roadblock is the mind.* The mind plays an important role in achieving every kind of success and goal—minor, everyday goals, and major goals.

The mind is like a young child who accepts, and takes for granted, whatever it sees or hears, without judgment and without considering the consequences.

We are constantly flooded with thoughts, ideas, and information coming through our five senses, other people, news media, and TV. These thoughts, ideas, and information penetrate the mind, whether we are aware of this process or not.

But you have the *power* to interrupt the pattern. You don't have to accept everything you think. Replace "I can't" with "I will," "I'm not" with "I am." When you convince yourself that you are ready to move forward, here's the motivating question, how badly do you want it? How badly do you want that promotion, that new house, that new job or relationship? When you want it badly enough, you'll do what it takes to get it. So the first step is finding the *why*. This is the principal behind every successful person and business. It becomes the driver that keeps the brain on track.

Ask yourself, *Why is it necessary for me to accomplish this? What will I become by achieving it? What will I gain?* Begin with *why* in mind, and you will achieve what you believe.

Choose Wisely

Someone said, "You must make a choice to take a chance or your life will never change. You have power. Choose to make changes, not excuses. Choose to be motivated, not manipulated. Choose to be useful, not used. To excel, not compete. Choose self-esteem, not self-pity. Choose to listen to your inner voice, not the random opinion of others."

Some choices we have made in life have led us on great travels, and other choices have caused traffic jams and detours. But here is the good news: *you are still here!* You are still alive, and that means you have the opportunity to have greater success in your future based on the choices you make.

Go get your blessing! Your destiny is a matter of choice. It is a thing to be achieved! Don't wait another day. Turn "I wish" into *"I will."*

You can become anyone you want to be and do anything you set your mind to accomplishing. It doesn't matter what happened to you. What matters is what you do next.

Begin outlining your first steps. Identify some goals to get you started. Make a decision to move forward—and don't worry about mistakes. They are simply proof that you are trying.

It's Done

Maintaining your motivation can be a difficult task. It's one of the top reasons people have trouble accomplishing goals. When we start a project, we're on fire! We are full of energy and excitement about the task ahead. But as time progresses, that fire starts to dim until there's barely a spark.

But you can win! To boost your motivation, instead of creating a to-do list, create an it's-done list! When you do *anything* you consider useful, however small it may be, write it down on your done list. At the end of the day, look over your list and celebrate everything you finished. Success is a process—*every* step forward is getting you closer to your goal.

Review your it's-done list regularly—in the mornings to kick start your day, or every week or month. Review it whenever you need a dose of perspective. Recognize that you may not be where you want to be, but you're surely on your way.

The simple act of pausing to reflect and acknowledge your efforts provides *valuable boosts of motivation, focus, and insight* that would otherwise be lost amid your busy day. Your done list acts as a signpost, a manifestation of all of that day's hard work. This flips an overwhelmed mindset into action mode to correct course, learn from mistakes, and ultimately *make better progress.*

Sooner than you know, your done list will be full and you will have accomplished your ultimate goal.

Midlife—No Strife

As you approach your forties and fifties, you may find that your friendships have dwindled away. It's a big change from the days when you were attending school or raising young children.

If you are experiencing the empty nest syndrome or transitioning through a divorce, you probably have more time on your hands and fewer daily commitments to focus on, leaving you feeling anxious and maybe even bored, believe it or not. This is the perfect time to reconnect with old friends and build new relationships so you don't have to move forward alone or in fear. Here are a few tips that were successful for me:

Tip 1. *Make a commitment to meet with friends.* Schedule that time on your calendar; it is just as important as following up with business clients. Video calls and texting are great, but they don't compare to sitting around the table together after dinner. Extend your personal and business travel to occasionally drop in and visit a friend.

Tip 2. *Collaborate on a project.* Pursue the same activities with friends, even when distance is a divide. You'll have plenty to talk about if you're both taking gourmet cooking classes or training for a charity run.

Tip 3. *Focus on quality relationships.* Having a few close friends beats having hundreds of followers on Facebook. Meaningful interactions far outweigh arbitrary popularity. In later life, you may find yourself happier enjoying more solitude while still treasuring occasions when you gather with loved ones.

Tip 4. *Exchange support.* Giving and taking is one of most important signs of a quality friendship. Move into your golden years with a circle of friends who serve as advisors, sounding boards, and cheerleaders.

At midlife, you still have plenty of fascinating years ahead and a lot more to achieve. Find friends to share in your experiences so that your future can be even greater than your past.

Side Hustle Muscle

I often receive questions from individuals who want to pursue a dream job but also must maintain other employment until the side hustle, for instance, an event planning business, becomes the main muscle. Although it will take time, energy, and planning, you don't have to leave your job while pursuing your dreams. In fact, I caution against that until you have saved money to support you until your planning business is profitable. Here are some things I suggest you can do to get started:

1. To be sure this is something you want to do full time, you should fully understand the business—find a mentor or business owner you can talk with to learn more about the responsibilities for event services.

2. Work part time to build the business. This means developing your strategy—determine your short-term and long-term goals, marketing your services, getting new clients, understanding

both the financial and personal investments necessary to operating and building your reputation.

3. Volunteer with nonprofit organizations to gain more experience. This is a good way to meet potential clients and improve your skills.

Before you jump into the water with both feet, you should understand the costs and benefits of pursuing your goals.

Consider the story of Michelle Newson, owner of Onederland Events. Newson is a busy and successful event planner based in Los Angeles, but her arrival wasn't without ups, downs, and a surprising number of multi-state moves. After just one semester in college, she was recruited to work in the Walt Disney College Program. A one-year experience turned into six years of learning in various departments including the wedding planning team. While in Florida, she completed her degree and ended up back and forth between New York and Florida before eventually moving back home with her parents in Chicago to start Onederland Events. A self-described risk-taker, Michelle said she wanted to be in control of her happiness.

She was on a great path in her corporate career, but it didn't matter because she wanted to put her own stamp on the world. But it wasn't easy. She recalls having tough times and often second-guessing herself. But a chance meeting at a bridal expo at a local church changed everything. She met an editor of a bridal magazine that wanted to produce an exclusive bridal show. The next day she had her first client and things took off from there.

Recognize that the costs might initially outweigh the benefits. Yet if it is your dream, your passion, and your purpose, you will find a way to make it work. Rome wasn't built in a day, and it's likely your business may not either.

The Perspective Objective

Do you have difficulty handling challenges? *With the right perspective, any situation can be handled effectively and with minimal drama.* Learning to direct your thoughts and attention are valuable assets in troubling times.

Maintaining a positive attitude provides the best opportunity of finding a solution. If you're forced to deal with a negative situation, why not do it with a smile? Use these strategies to keep a level head when everything is going wrong:

1. Find a way to learn from the challenge. Challenging times can be excellent learning opportunities. There's a lesson in there somewhere, but you must look for it. At the very least, ask yourself how you can prevent a similar situation from happening again. *Imagine how great life would be if you never repeated the same mistake twice!*

2. Ask yourself what you can do about it, then listen to the answers you receive. Stay focused on solutions and avoid dwelling on the problems. Worrying won't make it better.

3. Maintain a positive attitude. One challenging situation doesn't negate all the good things in life. Make a list of the many things that create a sense of gratitude in your life to generate feelings

that will increase your ability to overcome your circumstance.

4. Realize that the situation is temporary. You've had many challenging times in your life, but you've survived all of them. It's often surprising how much a situation can change in just a couple of days, weeks, or months. Just hang on!

5. Visualize a positive outcome. In many respects, you get what you expect. Take a few minutes each day and visualize a highly positive outcome.

It's not only *what* we go through but *how* we go through it that matters. Remember that the circumstances will eventually pass—and your perspective can make all the difference.

Cues for the Work Blues

Sadly, not everyone loves their job. A recent study shows that 70 percent of people polled were either somewhat or not satisfied at all with their work, proving that work can be challenging and pull the joy out of you. But it doesn't have to be that way.

To find more joy at work implement these strategies:

-   **Treat yourself for achieving goals.** You probably find yourself dragging through day to day tasks…groaning and unwillingly to tackle them. Try this approach: as you move through one task at a time, take a few moments of downtime for yourself. That may mean walking away from your desk or playing a few rounds of solitaire. Whatever it is, treat yourself to something you like.

- **Be positive.** Another way is to trick yourself is by being positive. You have the power of choice. Use it! Find a positive element in an unpleasant tasks. Recognize that each task gives you more work experience that you can use to land the job of your dreams!

- **Be a mentor.** Helping someone else succeed can bring you satisfaction and open your eyes to things you didn't realize about your work before. It's a win-win!

- **Focus on success.** This is a sure-fire way to encourage more joy in your work is to focus on success. Just like many other things in life, time is best spent focusing on where you want to go—not where you are. Focus on the successful end result instead of the monotony of the task.

Don't delay. Make today the day that you find more joy in your job and experience greater professional success!

Train Your Brain

It's said that "Life is 10 percent what happens to you and 90 percent how you react." Even in bad situations you can train your brain to see the positive in any situation. Achieve more by asking and answering these questions:

1. *Am I still breathing?* Sometimes the best we can do is breathe. During overwhelmingly difficult

times, our stress levels rise, our breathing gets shallow, and our body's natural rhythm gets all out of whack. One of the keys to staying positive is to be relaxed. Take a breath—don't stress!

2. Ask yourself, ***What is my part in this?*** Don't play the blame game. Acknowledge and accept your responsibility for the situation.

3. Ask, ***What is in my control?*** When life feels completely overwhelming, we often lose sight of those things we *can* change. Take action by honestly assessing your situation, look for things you *can* control. And do it!

4. Then ask yourself, ***What is out of my control?*** Whether it's other people, mother nature, or just plain bad timing, regardless of how much we want to, we can't control everything. Take time to look at your difficulty, identify the things that are out of your control, and then let them go. As a result, you'll gain clarity and decrease stress.

If you are able to accept, acknowledge, and assess your situation, you are on a path toward greater success. Your reaction can lead to positive attractions in your thoughts and relationships. Train your brain to see the good to get better!

Why Wait?

Every day the sun rises and sets and another day passes. Did you take a step toward attaining your goals and dreams today? Maybe you discovered something wonderful or really enjoyed yourself.

However, the other possibility is that the day slipped by pretty much unnoticed. Maybe days, weeks, or even months pass when you don't think about your personal goals. If that's the case, the question you have to ask yourself is, *What am I waiting for?*

Time waits for no one. But it's never too late to begin again. You can start working to achieve your personal and professional desires today. They're still there, just waiting for you!

To take control so you can live the life you desire:

- Review your desired goals and jot them down.

- Acknowledge you're worth it. Whatever time, research, and money it takes to work toward your goals, you deserve it. Recognize this fact and remind yourself of it regularly.

- Don't let another day go by without doing something to make progress toward your chosen wishes.

- Be sure to infuse aspects of your life goals into each day. Remind yourself daily about what you're doing, the progress you've made, and what you want to do next to get even closer to your dream.

- Don't wait on other people or situations to make your life "happen." Acknowledge that only you are in charge of your life. There's no elevator to success—you have to take the stairs.

Dream big! Set goals! Take action! Be fearless, inspired, and transformed for greater success.

9 to 5 Dreaming

Maybe you want to star in a Hollywood movie or tutor kids in South America. Meanwhile, you're spending your weeks sitting in a cubicle or chauffeuring your kids from one activity to another.

There's no need to envy risk-takers who drop it all to pursue their dreams. Plenty of people juggle family and business responsibilities while they write their novel at night or complete their MBA online.

Whether you take the fast track or a slower route, you can live out your dreams. Consider these five ideas for pursuing your passions without giving up your day job:

- **Plan your strategy.** Stable employment gives you time to map out your future. Figure out what training and networking you need to get from point A to point B.

- **Maintain structure.** Depending on your personality, a wide-open schedule could feel liberating—or overwhelming. Your routine may keep you prompt and punctual.

- On the other hand, you may just want to **supplement a job you love**. Your passion project could remain a side venture. Research ways to fulfill those endeavors on weekends.

- **Scale back.** If your job consumes your time and energy like a black hole, you may need to switch gears. Find balance by moving into a less-demanding position.

- **Look for areas of overlap.** Whatever you do for a living, you can probably identify your favorite tasks. Leveraging your strengths at work will lay a foundation for your own endeavors.

You can work 9 to 5 and keep your dream alive. Turn your current position into a resource that will help you learn to love what you do and do what you love.

Recognize and Strategize

Whether you realize it or not, you have incredible power to change your life. And while you may think you need a boss, spouse, partner, or any other person to make the change, you created the life you have now and you can take steps in creating a more fulfilling life.

Follow these three strategies to use your power to change your life:

The first step is to *take full responsibility* for all the good *and* challenging things in your life. Even if some of the things you wish to change aren't really your fault, it is still 100 percent your responsibility to change them. This is critical if you want your life to change.

Look at your past successes. Acknowledge the power you had in your accomplishments. And make note of the role you played in things that may not have turned out the way you wanted. Understand how you influenced the outcomes of your life.

Set new goals and reinforce them. Many people live like a feather blowing in the wind, never having a true direction. It's important to choose your destination. Leaving things to chance is choosing not to use your power. Each day, rewrite your goal and imagine how you'll feel when you accomplish it. It will become a priority over all the other noise in your head.

Everything that has happened in your life so far is the result of decisions you made. You've got the power to do whatever it is you want to do in life. Choose! Change! And achieve!

Tackle it or Take it

Along life's journey, we face situations that require us to make decisions if we want to live successfully. It could be a job situation, a relationship issue, or a feeling that causes low productivity, stagnation, or emotional discomfort.

Individuals seek coaching for improvement—to gain clarity and to enhance or improve their decision-making abilities to move forward in their lives. For example, a coaching client shared his struggles on the job. He enjoyed his work, but not the way things were being managed in the workplace. The boss did not recognize his contributions. Another client was frustrated with the lack of support she was receiving from her spouse with housework. And another client was challenged by feelings that often caused depression.

When seeking resolutions, there are generally two choices that will get you where you want to be: tackle it or take it. Both pathways are determined by the individual, based on his or her abilities, wants, and resources. Let's break it down:

- Tackling it is very similar to its football analogy. You've got to get hold of the issue and wrestle it down until it screams, "UNCLE!" This means resolving it to a point that is acceptable so it is no longer a barrier to growth.

- Take it means accept it. Accept that your husband will never put his socks in the laundry basket or that your wife will always ask twenty consecutive questions the minute you walk through the door, even before you take off your coat. Accept that it is okay to be sad at times, but that sadness doesn't have to run your life. In time, these things will have less and less affect on your well-being, if you truly surrender and accept.

Let the Weak Say I Am Strong

As a coach, I hear this statement time and time again: "I want to pursue my passion, but I just can't." Maybe that's what you are saying today. You want a life that's centered on the things that light you up, doing things that nurture your soul. You want to be great and live an amazing life filled with joy, passion, and fulfillment, but by now you know the timing will never be right.

So what do you do?

Life development coach Stephenie Zamora gives advice about how to build your life around your passion:

1. Commit 100 percent to becoming the person you're meant to be. This means you will go after this dream of yours with every ounce of energy you have. Committing 100 percent means reading, practicing, applying, or doing something

that moves you closer to your goal. You may even have to work at a job you don't like or something that just pays the bills but lets you leave when the day is over. That's okay. Remember, that's not your end. It's a means to your end.

2. Give yourself proper nourishment. Without healthy physical and emotional well-being, you're nothing. It is essential to your success to make sure that you move your body, fill your stomach with healthy foods, and spend time praying, meditating, and journaling. It is a *priority* to care for yourself.

3. Practice constantly. Constant practice is the key to mastering whatever it is you want to master in your life. I don't think there's a single great writer, speaker, chef, or others who started out at the top of their game. If your dream is to be a world-renown author, you had better be writing every day, reading books, practicing your craft, trying new things, and growing.

4. Surround yourself with the right team. Find people who are passionate like you are and will understand what you're going through as you move forward. They will cheer you on and keep you motivated when you've lost steam. No matter how strong or independent you may be, you need a support system when things get hard— because things will get hard.

Take action now. Be realistic. Expect miracles!

CONCLUSION

I was incredibly inspired that my dream of having a successful business was possible after watching a video of Will Smith—actor, producer, comedian, rapper, songwriter—talking about his journey to success. What's especially remarkable to me about Will Smith and why I find encouragement in his story is simple, we grew up in the same neighborhood, we were bussed to the same school in the 1970s, we played in the same park—Belmont Plateau—and I even attended parties at the Wynne in the 1980s where he performed. I saw the passion and fire and determination in him. I witnessed from close view how he grew and reached fame and success.

I started this journey of encouraging and empowering others by choice, not chance. I am a wife and mother and had a successful career. I was blessed with what could seem like everything a woman could want—a handsome, hard-working husband, beautiful home, nice cars, but as my children got older, I started to feel like something was still missing and I wasn't fulfilled by the things around me or in me.

I always felt I should be doing more; I was searching for my purpose. In 2008 when banks were failing and the economy was in an uproar, my company started laying off people and I decided to retire from Corporate America and begin my journey. I didn't have a plan but I had a vision. Over the next year, there was one song playing in heavy rotation in my mind, the words of James Cleveland singing, "I don't feel no ways tired. Nobody told me the road would be easy. I don't believe He brought me this far to leave me." And yes we faced some life-altering challenges as a family. One of which was a business failure. But during that time my relationship with God strengthened. I just kept going. Though I had failed. I knew I wasn't a failure.

I unretired from my corporate career and excitedly, in the evenings and on weekends or any other spare moment I could find, I continued to pursue my purpose. I was again excelling more in the workplace. I was happy, but I wasn't fulfilled. Because I knew there was more for me to accomplish beyond those brick walls. Then one day I experienced the breakthrough I was awaiting in an instant. I contracted with a marketing coach to assist with building my online brand and within weeks of our discussion, I was booking a flight to Atlanta for coaching school and I haven't looked back.

Today I am living in my dream. I found my purpose in life. I hope you find this book as a source of encouragement to pursue your passion to achieve your goals to live fulfilled!

ABOUT THE AUTHOR

ADREAN TURNER, the "Career Fulfillment Expert," is a certified career coach, speaker, professional development trainer, and business consultant. She leverages twenty-five years of experience in management, marketing, operations, teaching, and training to partner with individuals, entrepreneurs, and organizations to achieve their maximum potential.

Adrean hosts the "F.I.T. Tips for Success®" podcast that broadcasts on a local Philadelphia radio station and international channels. In addition to servicing business and private client accounts, she is a master coach with the Muse®, trainer for the TriCounty Community Network, instructor for Chambers of Commerce throughout Pennsylvania, and adjunct professor of Business at Alvernia University. Adrean is a highly regarded public speaker for women's groups, businesses, and nonprofit organizations.

Connect with Adrean today for private career coaching to change your career or improve the one you have to gain more fulfillment. Her technique of coaching, encouragement, and strategic planning provides clients with the tools to move from a mediocre outlook of success to a magnificent vision of opportunities and achievement. This effective program draws on Adrean's proven six-step model for transforming your worklife and career aligns with what you want, and brings greater fulfillment, success, and reward.

Adrean's coaching program will guide you through rigorous self-discovery methods, hands-on learning techniques, and specific strategies that enable you to figure out how to maximize your power and potential to achieve the success you desire.

For information about coaching, speaking, or workshop services, visit www.coachadrean.com or call 415-237-3268. You can also sign up for a free consultation or her weekly newsletter loaded with inspiration, events, and advice.

Email: info@coachadrean.com

Phone: 415-237-3268

Website: http://coachadrean.com

ACKNOWLEDGMENTS

I would like to thank Lisa Blain who attended my very first coaching seminar and encouraged her husband, Fred Blain, General Manager of the Gospel Highway 11, 1110AM Philadelphia radio station to contact me which led to the creation of F.I.T. Tips for Success. To Fred Blain, the producer of F.I.T. Tips, thank you for the endless hours you spent helping me to develop content to engage audiences. You believed in my work at the beginning and provided honest advice to make me work hard to be a better writer and author. Thank you to Robyn McCollum, who provided technical support and social media guidance. Your support with syndication is priceless.

To everyone within the TriCounty Community Network and the Pottstown Area Health and Wellness Foundation: It's an honor to serve in the community with you. Some of the themes in this book came from my engagements training esteemed professionals within the member organizations and our brain storming sessions on workforce development strategies.

I also want to recognize Shawn Doyle, a mentor and friend, and exceptional speaker and coach who introduced me to Sound Wisdom enabling this opportunity to share my gifts with the world.

To the staff of Sound Wisdom: Thank you for your support and inspiration throughout the process. You are greatly appreciated!